POWERPOINT 2002

Copyright - Editions ENI - June 2002
ISBN: 2-7460-1628-1
Original edition: 2-7460-1426-2

Editions ENI

BP 32125
44021 NANTES Cedex 1

Tél. 02.51.80.15.15
Fax 02.51.80.15.16

e-mail : editions@ediENI.COM
http://www.editions-eni.com

English edition by Adrienne TOMMY
Collection directed by Corinne HERVO

MOUS
PowerPoint 2002

This logo is your guarantee that you are using a Microsoft®-approved preparation guide for the Microsoft® Office User Specialist PowerPoint 2002 exam.

This complete preparation guide provides you with the theory that explains all the features tested in the exam and practical exercises that you can work through, to find out how much you really know. When you can work through all these exercises, successfully and easily, you are ready to take the MOUS exam. At the end of the book, there is a list of all the PowerPoint 2002 exam objectives and the lesson number and exercise that relate to each objective.

For further information on the titles in the MOUS collection, visit the ENI Publishing Web site, at www.eni-publishing.com; click the **Catalogue** link and then click the **MOUS** link in the list of ENI collections.

What is the MOUS certification ?

The MOUS (Microsoft Office User Specialist) exam gives you the opportunity to obtain a meaningful certification, recognised by Microsoft®, for the Office applications: Word, Excel, Access, PowerPoint, and Outlook. This certification guarantees your level of skill in working with these applications. It can provide a boost to your career ambitions, as it proves that you can use effectively all the features of the Microsoft Office applications and thus offer a high productivity level to your employer. In addition, it is a certain plus when job-seeking: more and more companies require employment candidates to be MOUS certificate holders.

What are the applications concerned?

You can gain MOUS certification in Word 97 and Excel 97 as well as the Office 2000 and Office XP applications: Word, Excel, Access, Powerpoint and Outlook. For Word 97 and Excel 97, only one level exists. However, there are two levels available for Word 2000, Excel 2000, Word 2002 and Excel 2002, consisting of a Core level, for basic skills and an advanced Expert level. If you obtain the Expert level for Word and Excel as well as MOUS certification in PowerPoint, Access and Outlook (Office 2000 or XP), you are certified as a Master.

How do you apply to sit the exams?

To enrol for the exams, you should contact one of the Microsoft Authorized Testing Centers (or ATC). A list of these centres is available online at this address: http://www.mous.net. Make sure you know the version of the Office application for which you wish to obtain the certificate (is it the 97, 2000 or 2002 version?).

There is an enrolment fee for each exam.

On the day of the exam, you should carry some form of identification and, if you have already sat a MOUS exam, your ID number.

What happens during the MOUS exam?

During the exam, you will have your own computer, on which you must perform a series of set tasks in the application concerned. Each action required to perform each task is tested, to ensure that you have done exactly what you were asked to do.

You are allowed no notes, books, pencils or calculators during the exam. You can consult the application help, but you should be careful not to exceed the exam's time limit.

Each exam is timed; it lasts in general between 45 minutes and one hour.

How do you pass the exam?

You must carry out a certain percentage of the required tasks correctly, within the allocated time. This percentage varies depending on the exam.

You will be told your result as soon as you have finished your exam. These results are confidential (the data are coded) and are only made known to the candidate and to Microsoft.

What happens then?

You will receive a Microsoft-approved exam certificate, proving that you hold the specified MOUS (Microsoft Office User Specialist) level.

What happens if I fail?

You can take the exam as many times as you like, but will have to pay the enrolment fee again each time you apply.

How this book works

This book is the ideal companion to an effective preparation of the **MOUS PowerPoint 2002** exam. It is divided into several sections, each containing one or more **chapters**. Each section deals with a specific topic: managing presentations and slides, inserting and formatting text, using design templates and template elements, creating and editing drawing objects, tables, pictures, multimedia items and charts, working with slide shows and animations, exchanging data (working with other applications, in workgroups and on the Web). Each chapter is independent from the others. You can tailor the training to suit you: if you already know how to edit text, for example, you can skip this lesson and go straight to the practice exercise for that chapter, then if you feel you need some extra theory, you can look back at the relevant points in the lesson. You can also study the lessons and/or work through the exercises in any order you wish.

At the end of the book, there is an **index** to help you find the explanations for any action, whenever you need them.

From theory...

Each chapter starts with a **lesson** on the theme in question and the lesson is made up of a variable amount of numbered topics. The lesson should supply you with all the theoretical information necessary to acquire that particular skill. Example screens to illustrate the point discussed enhance the lesson and you will also find tips, tricks and remarks to complement the explanations provided.

...To practice

Test your knowledge by working through the **practice exercise** at the end of each chapter: each numbered heading corresponds to an exercise question. A solution to the exercise follows. These exercises are done using the documents on the CD-ROM accompanying the book, that you install on your own computer (to see how, refer to the INSTALLING THE CD-ROM instructions). In addition to the chapter exercises, six **summary exercises** dealing with each of the section themes are included at the end of the book. The solutions to these exercises appear as documents on the CD-ROM.

All you need to succeed!

When you can complete all the practice exercises without any hesitation or problems, you are ready to sit the MOUS exam. In the table of contents for each chapter, the topics corresponding to a specific exam objective are marked with this symbol: 🏢. At the back of the book, you can also see **the official list of the PowerPoint 2002 exam objectives** and for each of these objectives the corresponding lesson and exercise number.

Free online training

Editions ENI have developed a series of practice tests for certain MOUS exams. These tests are free and can be found on the www.moustest.com site. These tests take place online, within the application in question, just like in the official exam. To use this, you need an Internet connection on your computer, the application (e.g. Word 2002) and Internet Explorer 5.0 or later. At the end of the test, you can see your results in detail.

The layout of this book

This book is laid out in a specific way with special typefaces and symbols so you can find all the information you need quickly and easily:

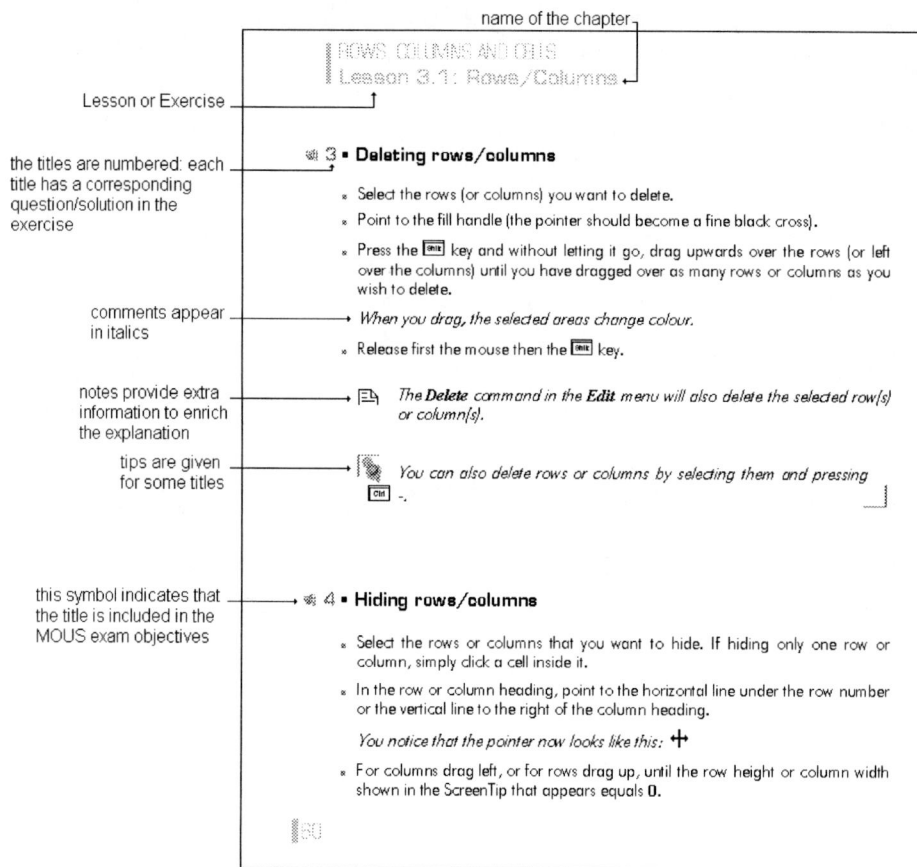

name of the chapter

ROWS COLUMNS AND CELLS
Lesson 3.1: Rows/Columns

Lesson or Exercise

the titles are numbered: each title has a corresponding question/solution in the exercise

3 ▪ Deleting rows/columns

- Select the rows (or columns) you want to delete.
- Point to the fill handle (the pointer should become a fine black cross).
- Press the [Shift] key and without letting it go, drag upwards over the rows (or left over the columns) until you have dragged over as many rows or columns as you wish to delete.

comments appear in italics → *When you drag, the selected areas change colour.*

- Release first the mouse then the [Shift] key.

notes provide extra information to enrich the explanation → *The **Delete** command in the **Edit** menu will also delete the selected row(s) or column(s).*

tips are given for some titles → *You can also delete rows or columns by selecting them and pressing [Ctrl] -.*

this symbol indicates that the title is included in the MOUS exam objectives → **4 ▪ Hiding rows/columns**

- Select the rows or columns that you want to hide. If hiding only one row or column, simply click a cell inside it.
- In the row or column heading, point to the horizontal line under the row number or the vertical line to the right of the column heading.

You notice that the pointer now looks like this: ✛

- For columns drag left, or for rows drag up, until the row height or column width shown in the ScreenTip that appears equals 0.

You can tell whether an action should be performed with the mouse, the keyboard or with the menu options by referring to the symbol that introduces each action: 🖰, 🎲 and 📋.

Installing the CD-ROM

The CD-ROM provided contains the documents used to work through the practice and summary exercises and the summary exercise solutions. When you follow the installation procedure set out below, a folder called MOUS PowerPoint 2002 is created on your hard disk and the CD-ROM documents are decompressed and copied into the created folder.

* Put the CD-ROM into the CD-ROM drive of your computer.
* Right-click the **start** button and take the **Explore** option.
* In the left pane of the Explorer window, scroll through the list until the CD-ROM drive icon appears. Click this icon.

The contents of the CD-ROM appear in the right pane of the Explorer window. The documents used for the practice and summary exercises are compressed in the MOUS PowerPoint 2002.exe file, although they also exist in standard form in the Practice Exercises and Summary folders.

* Double-click the icon of the **MOUS PowerPoint 2002** folder in the right pane of the Explorer window.

*The **MOUS PowerPoint 2002** dialog box appears.*

* Click **Next**.

The installation application offers to create a folder called MOUS Power-Point 2002.

* Modify the proposed folder name if you wish then click **Next**. If several people are going to be doing the practice exercises on the same computer, you should modify the folder name so each person is working on their own copy of the folder.
* Click **Yes** to confirm creating the **MOUS PowerPoint 2002** folder.

The installation application decompresses the documents then copies them into the created folder.

* Click **Finish** when the copying process is finished.

* When the copy is finished, click the ☒ button on the **Explorer** window to close it.

   You can now put away the CD-ROM and start working on your MOUS exam preparation.

PRESENTATIONS AND SLIDES
Lesson 1.1: Presentations

1 ▪ Starting/leaving Microsoft PowerPoint 2002

* Click the **start** button on the taskbar.

* Drag the mouse pointer to the **All Programs** menu (or **Programs** if you are not using Windows XP).

* Click the **Microsoft PowerPoint** option.

The icon might be present on the Windows Desktop. If this is the case, double-click the icon to start PowerPoint.

The workscreen appears. What appears on your screen may not be exactly the same as on the illustration above.

There are two windows: the application window and the document (which is called a presentation in PowerPoint) window.

The application window

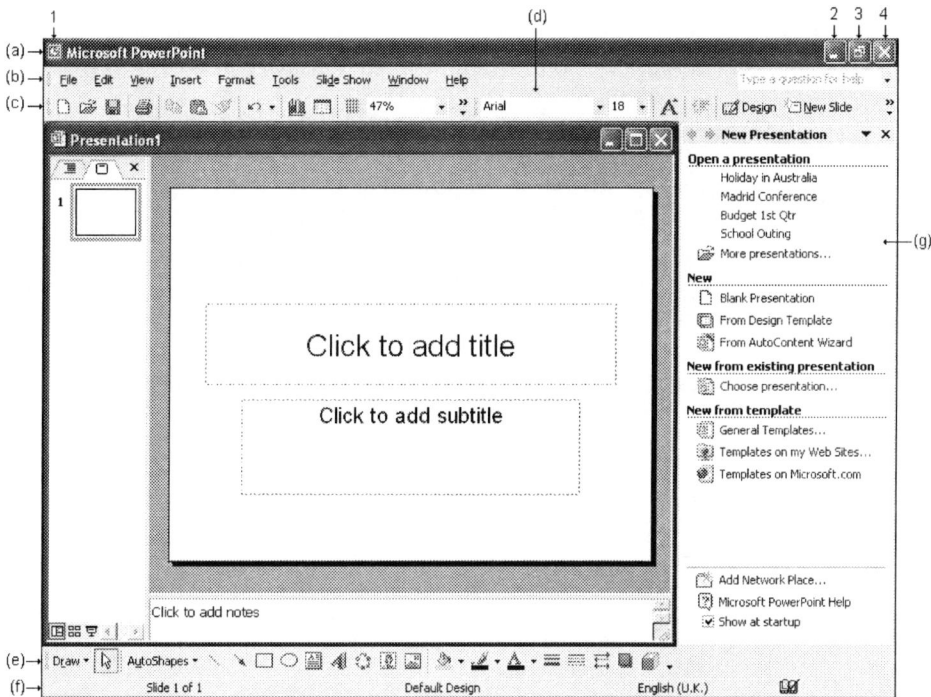

- The **title bar (a)**: on the left is the **Control** menu **(1)** followed by the name of the application (**Microsoft PowerPoint**) and, if the presentation window is maximized, the name of the active presentation. To the right you can see the **Minimize (2)**, **Restore (3)** and **Close (4)** buttons.

- The **menu bar (b)**: contains all the PowerPoint menus. Each menu contains a list of commands that are available as you work.

- The **toolbars (c)**, **(d)** and **(e)**: these contain the different tools so you can access the most frequently used commands quickly. The **Standard (c)** and **Formatting (d)** toolbars might share the same line. The **Drawing** toolbar **(e)** appears under the presentation window.

- The **status bar (f)**: it contains the number of the current slide followed by the total number of slides in the presentation, and the name of the template in use.

※ The **task pane (g)**: you can use this pane to carry out any of ten different actions, namely creating a presentation, using the Office Clipboard, finding various things, inserting a picture, applying slide layouts, choosing design templates, colour schemes and animation schemes, customising animations and applying slide transitions.

The presentation window

※ To separate the presentation window from the application window (as can be seen on the previous illustration), use the **Window - Arrange All** command.

※ By default the presentation window is in Normal view. This is made up of three panes: a pane containing **tabs (a)**, the **slide** pane **(b)** and the **notes** pane **(c)**. All of these panes can be resized by dragging their borders (the thick grey lines). Use F6 to go to the next pane or Shift F6 to go to the previous pane. You can also use the **Next Pane** option in the **Window** menu, or simply click in the pane you want.

- The **title bar (d)**: contains the **Control** menu **(1)**, the name of the active presentation, and the **Minimize (2)**, **Maximize (3)** and **Close (4)** buttons.
- The **views (e)**: these tool buttons are used to activate the view which is best adapted to the work you are doing.

1 2 3

1 - Normal view   3 - Slide Show

2 - Slide Sorter view

- The **scroll bars (f)**: use these bars to move around the length and breadth of the current view.

Leaving PowerPoint 2002

- **File - Exit** or ⊠ on the application window or Alt F4
- If you have made changes to the presentation but have not saved them, PowerPoint tells you and you can click:

  Yes   to save the changes and close PowerPoint.

  No   to close PowerPoint without saving the changes.

  Cancel   to neither save the changes nor leave PowerPoint.

2 ▪ Managing certain workscreen items

The task pane

- **View - Task Pane**

  The task pane also appears automatically when you carry out one of the ten actions described in the previous section.

PRESENTATIONS AND SLIDES
Lesson 1.1: Presentations

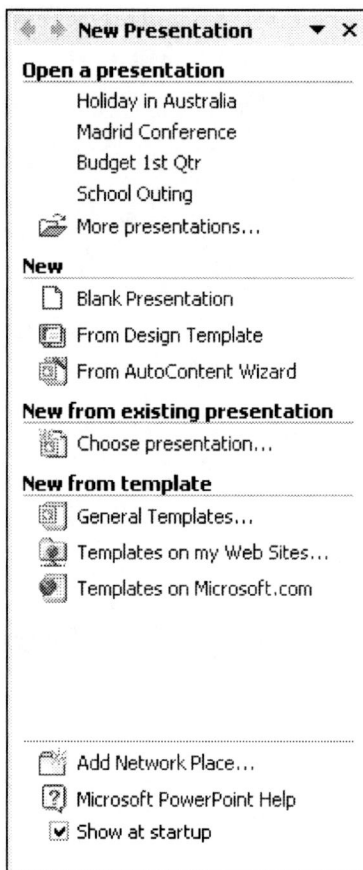

* To display a different task pane, open the ▼ list on its title bar and click the name of the pane you wish to use.

  The task pane's name appears on its title bar.

* To scroll through the panes in the order in which they have been used, click the ◆ or ➡ button on the pane title bar.

* To hide the task pane, click its close button ☒ or repeat the **View - Task Pane** command.

The Office Assistant

The Office Assistant follows your work and suggests solutions to your problems.

* To show the Office Assistant, you can use **Help - Show the Office Assistant** or [?] or [F1].

* To ask for help about a particular point, click the assistant, type a keyword and click **Search**.

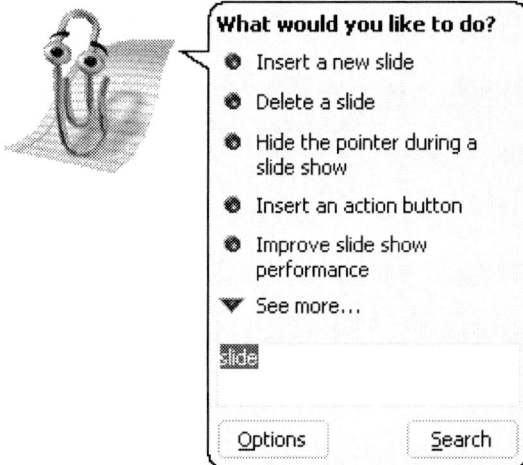

*Different topics that correspond to your search appear. The **See more** option, if it is present, leads to more help subjects.*

* Click the required topic to see the corresponding help text. Read the help text then click the [X] button to close the window.

* To hide the Office Assistant, use **Help - Hide the Office Assistant** or right-click the Assistant and take the **Hide** option.

A light bulb appears next to the Assistant when it has advice for you; simply click the Assistant to see the tip.

Toolbars

* **View - Toolbars** or right-click any toolbar on display.

In the list, some toolbar names are ticked; these are the bars currently on display. The toobars that are not ticked are hidden but available for use.

* Click the name of a toolbar to hide it, or display it.

Zoom

* In Normal view, click the pane whose magnification you wish to change.

* Open the `32%` list box on the **Standard** toolbar.

*The percentages available in this list depend on the current view. The **Fit** option, available in Notes Page and Normal view, asks PowerPoint to calculate the best zoom value to ensure that all the information can be seen on the screen.*

* Choose a preset zoom or type in your own value then press ⏎.

📄 *You can also use the **View - Zoom** menu.*

18

▦3 ▪ **Opening a presentation**

A presentation is a document created in PowerPoint.

▪ **File - Open** or [icon] or [Ctrl] **O**

▪ Indicate where the presentation is by clicking one of the buttons on the Places Bar (in the left of the dialog box) or by using the **Look in** drop-down list.

The **History** button leads to shortcuts to the documents/folders you have used recently. Click the **My Documents** button to see the contents of the **My Documents** folder. The **Desktop** button shows the shortcuts on the Windows Desktop. Click the **Favorites** button to open the **Favorites** folder. The **My Network Places** button opens access to saved network locations and can be used to browse your network (in some versions of Windows, this may be replaced by a **Web Folders** button, which opens a list of folders on Web servers).

In the **Look in** list you can see all the drives accessible on your computer (such as the floppy disk drive (A:), the hard disk (C:) and the CD-ROM drive).

▪ Select the drive that contains the presentation.

PRESENTATIONS AND SLIDES
Lesson 1.1: Presentations

A list of the folders on the selected drive appears, along with the documents in the current folder (if there are any).

⁎ Go to the folder that contains the presentation you want by double-clicking the folder icon.

⁎ To go to the folder above, click the 🔼 tool button; to go to the last folder you visited, click the ⬅ tool button.

⁎ To see a more detailed list of the folders and files, open the list on the 🔲 ▾ tool button and click the **Details** option.

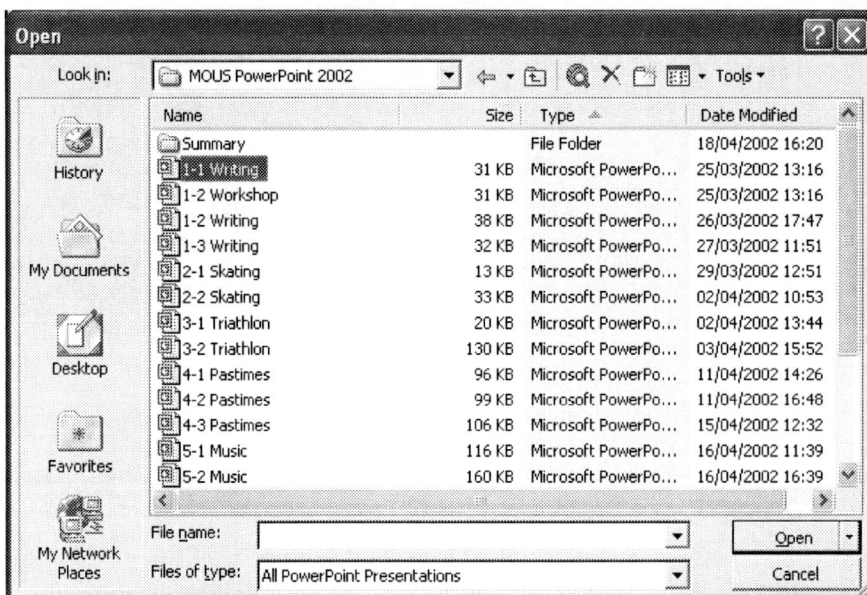

Open				
Look in:	MOUS PowerPoint 2002			Tools ▾
Name		**Size**	**Type** ▵	**Date Modified**
📁 Summary			File Folder	18/04/2002 16:20
1-1 Writing		31 KB	Microsoft PowerPo...	25/03/2002 13:16
1-2 Workshop		31 KB	Microsoft PowerPo...	25/03/2002 13:16
1-2 Writing		38 KB	Microsoft PowerPo...	26/03/2002 17:47
1-3 Writing		32 KB	Microsoft PowerPo...	27/03/2002 11:51
2-1 Skating		13 KB	Microsoft PowerPo...	29/03/2002 12:51
2-2 Skating		33 KB	Microsoft PowerPo...	02/04/2002 10:53
3-1 Triathlon		20 KB	Microsoft PowerPo...	02/04/2002 13:44
3-2 Triathlon		130 KB	Microsoft PowerPo...	03/04/2002 15:52
4-1 Pastimes		96 KB	Microsoft PowerPo...	11/04/2002 14:26
4-2 Pastimes		99 KB	Microsoft PowerPo...	11/04/2002 16:48
4-3 Pastimes		106 KB	Microsoft PowerPo...	15/04/2002 12:32
5-1 Music		116 KB	Microsoft PowerPo...	16/04/2002 11:39
5-2 Music		160 KB	Microsoft PowerPo...	16/04/2002 16:39

File name:		Open
Files of type:	All PowerPoint Presentations	Cancel

*The name of each document appears in the first column. The detailed list shows the **Size** of the documents, their **Type** and the date and time they were last modified.*

⁎ To see the properties of a particular presentation, select it then open the list on the 🔲 ▾ tool button and choose **Properties**.

* If you want to see a preview of the presentation, select it, open the list on the ▦▾ tool button and choose **Preview**.

  The first slide in the presentation appears in the right of the dialog box.

* To show the list of presentations as thumbnails (miniature pictures), open the list on the ▦▾ tool button and choose the **Thumbnails** option.

* To return to a simple list, click the **List** option in the list on the ▦▾ tool button.

* Open the required presentation(s) by double-clicking the name of the presentation or selecting the presentations with Shift-clicks or Ctrl-clicks then clicking **Open**.

  *When several presentations are open, you only see the last presentation opened; to activate a presentation that is open but hidden, open the **Window** menu and click its name.*

  *Before you start PowerPoint, if you know that you are going to be working on one of the last presentations used on your computer, you can use **Start - Documents** (or **Start - My Recent Documents**) on your Windows desktop and click the name of the presentation you want to open.*

  *While you are working in PowerPoint, if you want to open one of the last four presentations saved, open the **File** menu and, at the end of this menu, click the name of the presentation you want to open. The number of presentations available at the end of the **File** menu depends on the number of **entries** given for the **Recently used file list** option in the **Options** dialog box (**Tools - Options - General** tab). If the **New Presentation** task pane is open, you can also click one of the last four files used (in the **Open a presentation** section) or click the **More presentations** link to go to the **Open** dialog box.*

4 ▪ Changing the view

Normal view

* **View - Normal** or [⊞]

*This view is the default view and is used for creating slides. On its left side, it has a tabs pane containing two tabs (**Outline (a)** and **Slides (b)**). On the right, it displays the current slide's contents in the **slide pane (c)** (you can work on your slide in this pane). At the bottom of the window there is the **notes pane (d)**, which you can use to add comments to the active slide.*

* To see the slides as small pictures, click the **Slides** tab [▭].

You can work in this tab to move around rapidly within the presentation and/or to reorganise its contents (copy or move slides).

* To display and work on the presentation outline (its text), click the **Outline** tab ⬛.

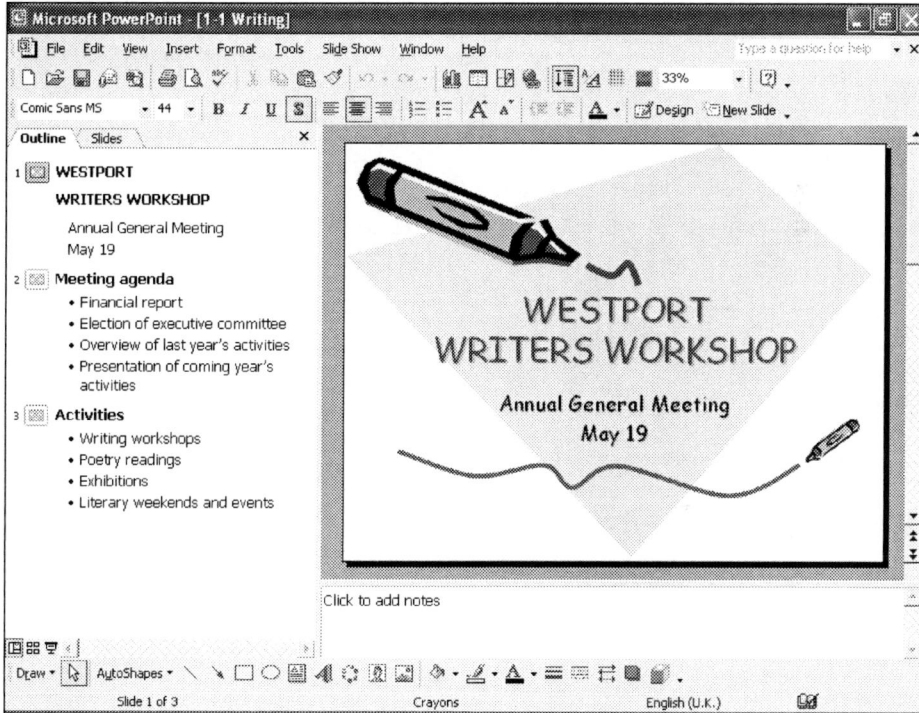

The tab names now appear. Beside each slide title you can see its number and a slide icon.

* To close the tabs pane, click its close button. If you want to display the tabs pane again, use **View - Normal (Restore Panes)** or click ⬛.

PRESENTATIONS AND SLIDES
Lesson 1.1: Presentations

Slide Sorter view

» **View - Slide Sorter** or ⊞

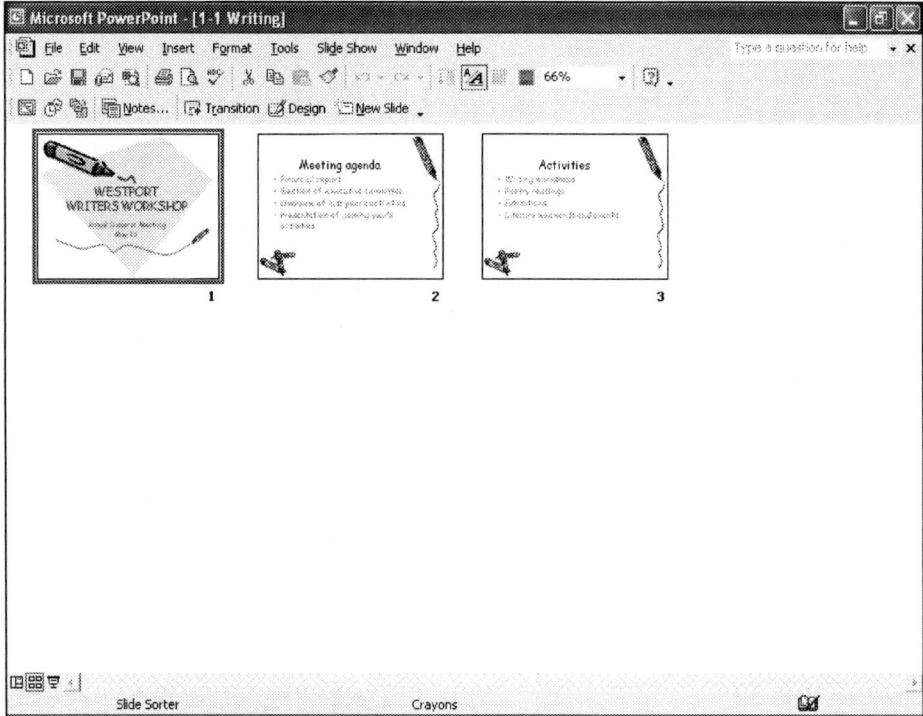

In this view you can see a miniature of all the slides in the presentation.
This view enables you to manage the slides (select, delete, copy and move them) with ease, and to add timings and animated transitions to the slides.
*A specific toolbar called the **Slide Sorter** toolbar appears underneath or next to the **Standard** toolbar.*

» To hide the formatting in Slide Sorter view, click the ⬛ tool button on the **Standard** toolbar.

When this tool is deactivated, all the text, graphics and formatting applied to the slides are hidden, leaving only the titles visible.

» To see the formatting again, click the same tool button again.

24

Notes Page view

» **View - Notes Page**

In this view you can enter comments about a slide more easily as the slide's notes pane appears much bigger on the screen.

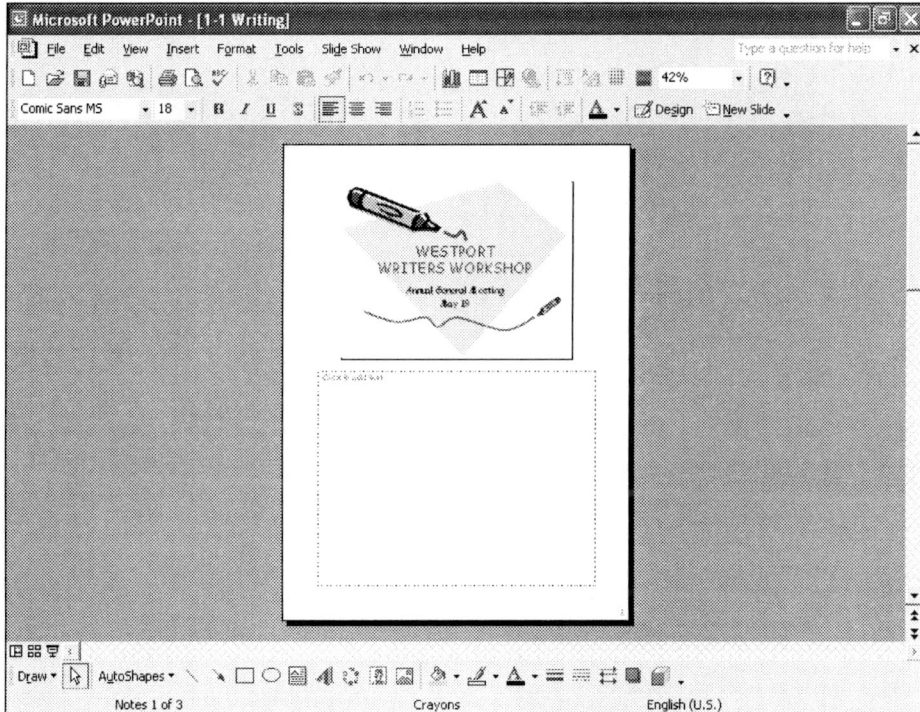

You can also type comments in the notes pane in **Normal** view.

A fast way to return to **Normal** view from **Slide Sorter** or **Notes Page** view is to double-click the slide.

⬛5 ▪ **Closing a presentation**

- **File - Close** or ❌ on the presentation window or ⌷Ctrl⌷ **W**

- If you have made changes without saving them, PowerPoint alerts you and you can click:

  Yes   to save and close the presentation.

  No   to close the presentation without saving the last changes.

  Cancel   to neither save the changes nor close the presentation.

⬛6 ▪ **Creating a blank presentation**

- Click the 🗋 tool button or use ⌷Ctrl⌷ **N**.

  *This action creates a presentation based on the **Default Design**, whose name appears on the status bar. The **Slide Layout** task pane opens at the same time.*

- Continue creating your presentation.

⬛7 ▪ **Creating a presentation with the AutoContent Wizard**

  This wizard helps you to create the structure of a presentation and to present its different ideas. It provides your presentation with a template and text suggestions.

- **File - New**

- In the **New Presentation** task pane that opens, click the **From AutoContent Wizard** link in the **New** section.

  The Office Assistant may offer to help you.

- If necessary, answer the question that the Office Assistant asks you.

- Click the **Next** button.

- Click a button to choose a **Presentation type** and choose a subtype in the right hand list.

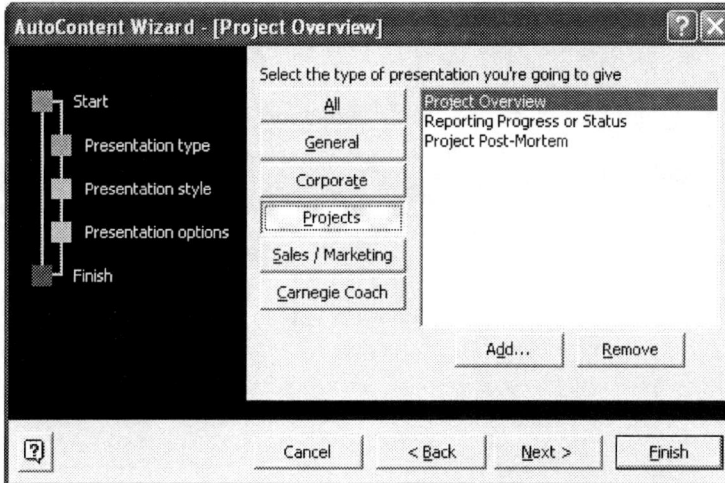

AutoContent Wizard - [Project Overview]

Select the type of presentation you're going to give

Start

Presentation type

Presentation style

Presentation options

Finish

All
General
Corporate
Projects
Sales / Marketing
Carnegie Coach

Project Overview
Reporting Progress or Status
Project Post-Mortem

Add...   Remove

Cancel   < Back   Next >   Finish

- Click the **Next** button.
- Give the **Presentation style**: **On-screen presentation**, **Web presentation**, **Black and white overheads**, **color overheads** or **35mm slides**.
- Click the **Next** button.
- Fill in the title and options offered.
- Click **Next** then **Finish**.
- Complete your presentation by inserting your own text and images.

8 ▪ Saving a presentation

- **File - Save** or 🖫 or Ctrl **S**

   *As you are saving a new presentation which does not yet have a name, the **Save As** dialog box appears. The buttons in this dialog box are the same as those in the **Open** dialog box.*

PRESENTATIONS AND SLIDES
Lesson 1.1: Presentations

* Type the **File name** you want to give the presentation.

  You can use up to 255 characters, including spaces.

* If you need to, you can use the **Save in** list or the buttons on the Places Bar to choose the drive on which you want to save the presentation.

* Go to the folder you want by double-clicking its folder icon.

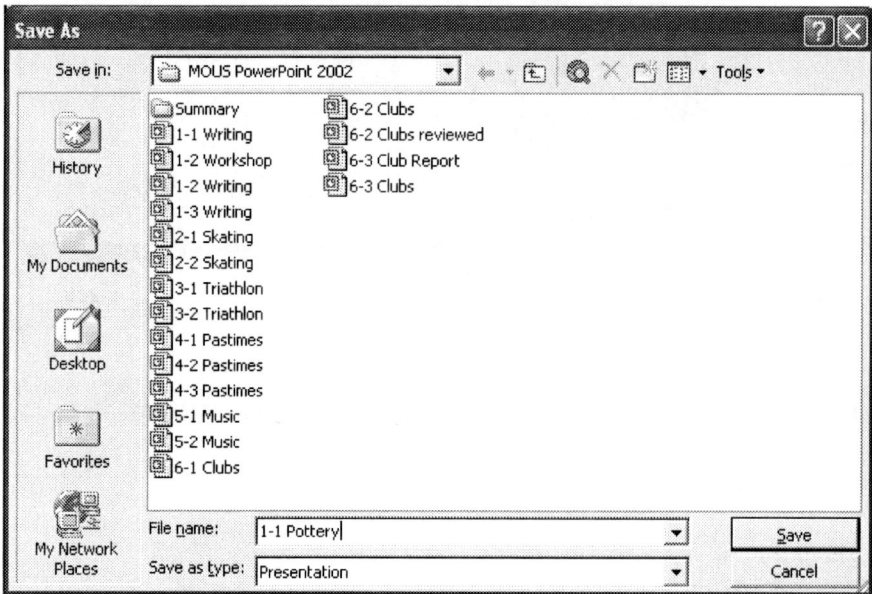

Use the [icon] tool button to create a new folder in the active folder.

* Click **Save**.

The presentation's name appears on its title bar. PowerPoint presentations have the extension .ppt, even if you cannot see this on your computer.

> *To define the default working folder, activate the **Tools - Options** command, click the **Save** tab then enter the file path for your working folder in the **Default file location** box.*

*To save an existing presentation, use the **File - Save** command or click or use the* Ctrl *S shortcut key.*

▯9 ▪ Creating a new presentation using a template

▪ Open the **New Presentation** task pane or use **File - New**.

*If you use the **File - New** command, the **New Presentation** task pane opens automatically. The **Blank Presentation** option (under **New**) creates a presentation using the default template.*

▪ In the **New Presentation** task pane, click the **From Design Template** link, under **New**.

*The **Slide Design** task pane appears.*

▪ In the **Apply a design template** section, click the type of design you want to apply to your presentation.

When you point to each template, its name appears in a ScreenTip.

PRESENTATIONS AND SLIDES
Lesson 1.1: Presentations

In the task pane, the templates are divided into three categories: *Used in This Presentation*, *Recently Used* and *Available For Use*.

※ Finish creating your presentation.

📄 *The names of the last templates used appear under* **New from template** *on the* **New Presentation** *task pane: to use one of these to create a new presentation, click the corresponding link.*

You can also create a new presentation using a template from the Web. You can use a template stored in a Web folder or on a Web site, using the **Templates on my Web Sites** *link on the* **New Presentation** *task pane or go and find a template on the Microsoft Office Web site with the* **Templates on Microsoft.com** *link.*

If you want to see all the available templates in a dialog box, click the **General Templates** *link under* **New from template** *on the* **New Presentation** *task pane.*

10 ▪ Saving a presentation including the fonts

This technique stores the TrueType fonts used with the presentation when you save it. This ensures that the presentation can be opened and printed correctly even if the user does not have all the fonts installed on his/her machine.

▪ For a new presentation, use the **File - Save** command then proceed as usual (give a **File name** and choose a folder to save in); for an existing presentation, use **File - Save As**.

▪ Open the list on the **Tools** button and click the **Save Options** option.

▪ Activate the **Embed TrueType fonts** option.

▪ Choose to **Embed characters in use only** or to **Embed all characters**.

▪ Click **OK** to close the **Save Options** dialog box.

- Click the **Save** button.

11 ▪ Using the Pack and Go Wizard

Packaging a presentation

- Prepare one or more formatted floppy disks.

- If necessary, save the presentation(s) you want to package.

- **File - Pack and Go**

The first step of the Pack and Go Wizard opens. If the Office Assistant asks whether or not you need help with this feature, answer its question according to your needs.

- Click the **Next** button.

- Decide whether you are packaging the **Active presentation** or **Other presentation(s)** (in which case, you can browse for the required files).

- Click the **Next** button.

* Choose where you want to copy the packaged file: to a floppy disk, another workstation or another folder (in which case, use **Choose destination**). If using a floppy disk, insert it into the drive. If you activate the **Choose destination** option, enter the name of the required folder or use the **Browse** button to create it or select it. In this case a dialog box opens, which resembles the **Save As** dialog box.

* Click the **Next** button.

* Indicate whether you wish to **Include linked files** (such as sounds, videos, other presentations) and/or **Embed TrueType fonts**.

* Click the **Next** button.

* If the workstation to which you are copying the packaged presentation does not have PowerPoint, you can choose to include the **Viewer for Microsoft Windows**. If this option is unavailable, the viewer is not installed on your own computer: click the **Download the Viewer** button to install it first. If you do not need the viewer, keep the **Don't include the Viewer** option active.

* Click the **Next** button.

The wizard explains what actions it will perform.

* Click the **Finish** button.

You may see a message asking you to install an additional component. If this happens, insert the PowerPoint 2002 or Microsoft Office XP CD-ROM in your drive and follow the instructions.

Unpackaging a presentation

* If you are viewing the presentation on another computer, open the Windows Explorer on that computer.

* If necessary, create a folder in which to unpackage the compressed files and the viewer.

* Go to the contents of the floppy disk or the folder (depending on where you saved the packaged presentation).

* Double-click the **Pngsetup.exe** file.

* Indicate the folder into which you intend to unpackage the compressed files.
* Click **OK** to confirm your choice.

* When the presentation has been unpackaged, choose whether or not you wish to view the presentation immediately.

Showing a slide show with the viewer

* Using the Windows Explorer, go to the folder into which you unpackaged the presentation containing the viewer.
* Double-click the **Ppview32.exe** file (this is the viewer file).
* Using the **Look in** list, go to the folder containing the unpackaged presentation.

  The viewer lists all the unpackaged files found and displays certain options pertaining to the slide show.

* Double-click the name of the presentation you wish to show.

  The slide show starts almost immediately.

* Go through the slide show.

  When the slide show has finished, the viewer returns to the foreground.

* When you have finished with the viewer, click the **Exit** button.

Below you can see **Practice Exercise** 1.1. This exercise is made up of 11 steps. If you do not know how to do one of the steps, go back to the title that corresponds to that particular lesson. When you have finished, you can check your work by reading the **Solution** that follows.

Steps that are likely to be tested during the MOUS exam are marked with this symbol: 🖪. However, it is a good idea to complete the whole exercise to ensure you have understood everything covered in the lesson.

👉 Practice Exercise 1.1

1. Start the Microsoft PowerPoint 2002 application.

2. Hide the Office Assistant, if it appears; make sure the task pane and the **Standard**, **Formatting** and **Drawing** toolbars are on display (all the other toolbars must be hidden). Activate **Fit** as the active zoom option.

🖪 3. Open the **1-1 Writing.ppt** presentation, which is in the **MOUS PowerPoint 2002** folder.

4. In Normal view, activate the **Outline** tab; next, go to **Notes Page** view.

🖪 5. Close the **1-1 Writing.ppt** presentation. If PowerPoint prompts you to save your changes, do not save them.

🖪 6. Create a new blank presentation.

🖪 7. Create a new presentation using the **AutoContent Wizard**. Choose **Project Overview** as the type of presentation and **On-screen presentation** as the style. As the presentation title, enter the text **Westport Pottery Workshop**.

🖪 8. Save the presentation you just created (with the AutoContent Wizard) under the name **1-1 Pottery**, saving it in the **MOUS PowerPoint 2002** folder.

🖪 9. Create a new presentation using the design template called **Capsules.pot**.

PRESENTATIONS AND SLIDES
Exercise 1.1: Presentations

⊞10. Save the presentation you just created into the **MOUS PowerPoint 2002** folder, calling it **1-1 Collection**. Embed the TrueType fonts as you save it.

⊞11. Use the **Pack and Go Wizard** to package the **1-1 Collection** presentation you just created. Create a new folder called **Presentations to go** within the **MOUS PowerPoint 2002** folder and save the packaged presentation into that folder. Do not include linked files but you should embed the TrueType fonts. You do not need to include the Viewer with the package.
To finish, save and close the **1-1 Collection** presentation.

If you want to put what you have learnt into practice on a real document, you can work on summary exercise 1 for the PRESENTATIONS AND SLIDES section, that you can find at the end of this book.

It is often possible to perform a task in several different ways, but here only the easiest solution is presented. You can go back to the corresponding lesson if you want to see other techniques you could use.

Solution to Exercise 1.1

1. To start PowerPoint, click the **Start** button on the taskbar, point to the **Programs** option (or **All Programs** if you are using Windows XP) and click **Microsoft PowerPoint**.

2. To hide the Office Assistant, right-click it with the mouse and choose the **Hide** option.
   If the task pane is not open, use the **View - Task Pane** command.

   To display only the Standard, Formatting and Drawing toolbars, open the **View** menu, take the **Toolbars** option and in the list, make sure that the **Standard**, **Formatting** and **Drawing** options are active. If not, activate them and make sure that none of the other toolbars is ticked (take care, as the Task Pane option also appears here; if you deactivate it you will close the task pane!).

   To choose a zoom level that will fit the slide neatly within the window, open the `32%` list on the **Standard** toolbar and choose the **Fit** option.

3. To open the 1-1 Writing.ppt presentation in the MOUS PowerPoint 2002 folder, click the tool button. Open the **Look in** list and choose the drive onto which you copied the documents from the CD-ROM provided with this book. Double-click the **MOUS PowerPoint 2002** folder then double-click the **1-1 Writing.ppt** presentation.

4. To activate the Outline tab while in Normal view, click the ▤ tab that appears in the tabs pane at the left of the screen. To go to Notes Page view, use the **View - Notes Page** command.

5. To close the 1-1 Writing.ppt presentation, use the **File - Close** command. If PowerPoint asks if you want to save your changes, click **No**.

6. To create a blank presentation, use ⌨Ctrl **N**.

7. To create a new presentation using the AutoContent Wizard use **File - New**. Click the **From AutoContent Wizard** link in the **New** section of the **New Presentation** task pane. Click the **Next** button.
At the **Presentation type** step, click the **Projects** button and select the **Project Overview** option then click **Next**.
At the **Presentation style** step, leave the **On-screen presentation** choice then click **Next**. In the **Presentation title** box, enter **Westport Pottery Workshop**, click **Next** then click **Finish**.

8. To save the AutoContent Wizard presentation you just created into the MOUS PowerPoint 2002 folder under the name 1-1 Pottery.ppt, click the 💾 tool button. Type **1-1 Pottery** in the **File name** text box.

If you need to, open the **Save in** drop-down list and select the drive on which the MOUS PowerPoint 2002 folder is stored. Double-click the **MOUS PowerPoint 2002** folder to open it then click the **Save** button.

9. To create a presentation based on the Capsules.pot template, use the **File - New** command to show the **New Presentation** task pane (if it is not already on the screen). Click the **From Design Template** link under **New**. In the **Apply a design template** frame, click the template called **Capsules.pot**.

🏮10.To save the presentation you just created into the MOUS PowerPoint 2002 folder, calling it 1-1 Collection and embedding its fonts, use the **File - Save** command. Check that you are saving into the **MOUS PowerPoint 2002** folder, then in the **File name** box, enter **1-1 Collection**.

On the dialog box, open the list on the **Tools** button and choose **Save Options**. Click the **Embed TrueType fonts** check box and activate the **Embed all characters (best for editing by others)** option, if necessary. Click **OK** then click the **Save** button.

🏮11.To use the Pack and Go Wizard, use the **File - Pack and Go** command. At the first step of the wizard, click **Next**. Leave the **Active presentation** option active then click **Next**. Activate the **Choose destination** option then click the **Browse** button, to package the presentation into a folder that you have yet to create.

If necessary, open the **Look in** list and select the drive on which the MOUS PowerPoint 2002 folder is stored then double-click the **MOUS PowerPoint 2002** folder to open it. Click the tool button and give **Presentations to go** as the folder name and confirm with **OK**.

Click the **Select** button on the **Choose Directory** dialog box.
Click **Next** on the Pack and Go Wizard.
Deactivate the **Include linked files** option and activate the **Embed TrueType fonts** option then click **Next**.
If necessary, activate the **Don't include the Viewer** option then click **Next** and finally **Finish**.

If PowerPoint asks you to install an additional component, click **Yes**, insert the appropriate CD-ROM and follow the instructions.

To save and close the 1-1 Collection presentation, use **File - Close** and if PowerPoint prompts you to save the presentation, click **Yes**.

PRESENTATIONS AND SLIDES
Exercise 1.1: Presentations

PRESENTATIONS AND SLIDES
Lesson 1.2: Slides

PRESENTATIONS AND SLIDES
Lesson 1.2: Slides

1 ▪ Moving around the slides

These techniques apply to the Normal and Notes Page views.

Going from one slide to another

▪ Click ⏶ on the vertical scroll bar or press `PgUp` to go to the previous slide.

▪ Click ⏷ or press `PgDn` to go to the next slide.

Going to a particular slide

▪ Drag the scroll cursor in the vertical scroll bar upward or downward.

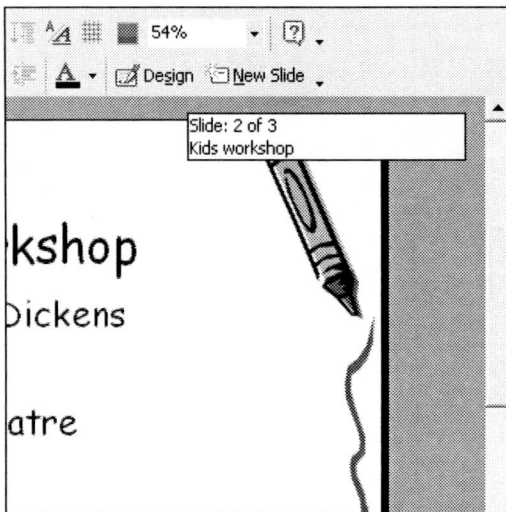

The number of the slide, followed by the total number of slides, is shown in a ScreenTip, along with the slide title.

▪ When you can see the name and number of the slide you want, release the mouse button.

▪ In Normal view, you can go to a slide by clicking the picture of it in the **Slides** tab or by clicking the slide text in the **Outline** tab.

▪ You can also go to the first slide in a presentation with the `Home` key or the last slide with the `End` key, providing you are not in a text placeholder.

42

2 ▪ Selecting slides

*The **Slides** tab in Normal or Slide Sorter view must be active.*

Selecting adjacent slides

▪ Click the first slide or slide thumbnail that you want to select.

▪ Hold down the [Shift] key.

▪ Click the last slide or slide thumbnail in the group.

*You can also use the **Outline** tab to select adjacent slides: click the slide number or icon to the left of the slide title to select it.*

Selecting non-adjacent slides

▪ Click one of the slides or slide thumbnails you wish to include in the selection.

▪ Hold down the [Ctrl] key.

▪ Click each of the other slides you wish to select.

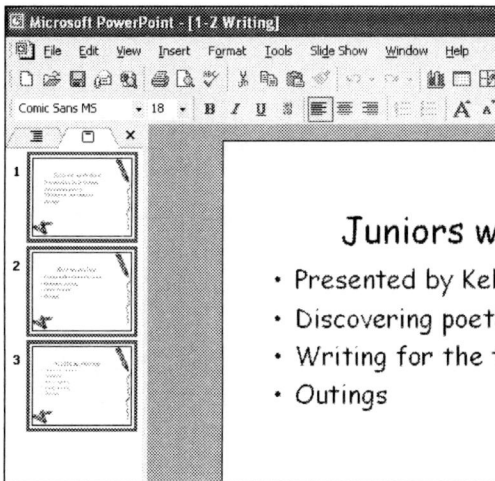

Selected slides have a thicker outline.

📄 *If you select a slide by mistake, you can remove it from the current selection with a [Ctrl]-click.*

📌 *To select all the slides in the presentation, click the **Slides** tab in Normal view and use **Edit - Select All** or [Ctrl] **A**.*

🪟3 ▪ Changing the layout of slides

※ If necessary, select the slides whose layout you wish to change.

※ Open the **Slide Layout** task pane or use **Format - Slide Layout**.

The **Slide Layout** task pane now appears on the screen, if it was not already on display.

PowerPoint offers you a choice of layouts, depending on the slide contents, and sorts the layouts by category: **Text Layouts** for slides that contain only placeholders, **Content Layouts** for slides containing objects such as tables, charts, pictures, diagrams and so on, **Text and Content Layouts** and **Other Layouts**.

* Point to the layout you wish to use.

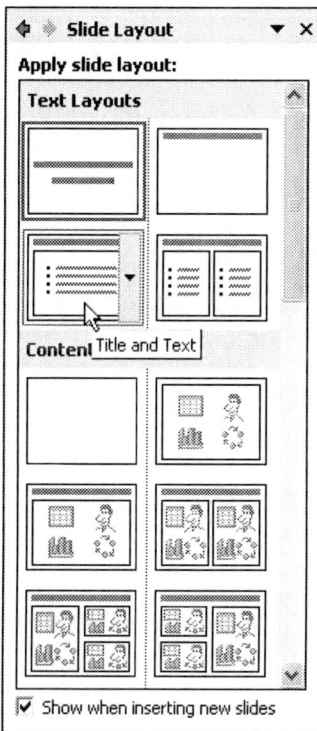

The name of that layout appears in a ScreenTip.

* Click the layout you decide to apply.

> PowerPoint automatically rearranges the items on the slide to suit the new layout you have applied.

🖳4 ▪ Creating a slide

* Activate the slide after which you wish to create the new slide or, if you want to create a new slide at the beginning of the presentation, click above the first slide in the **Slides** tab, in Normal view (a horizontal line will flash, representing the insertion point).

* **Insert - New Slide** or [New Slide] or [Ctrl] **M**

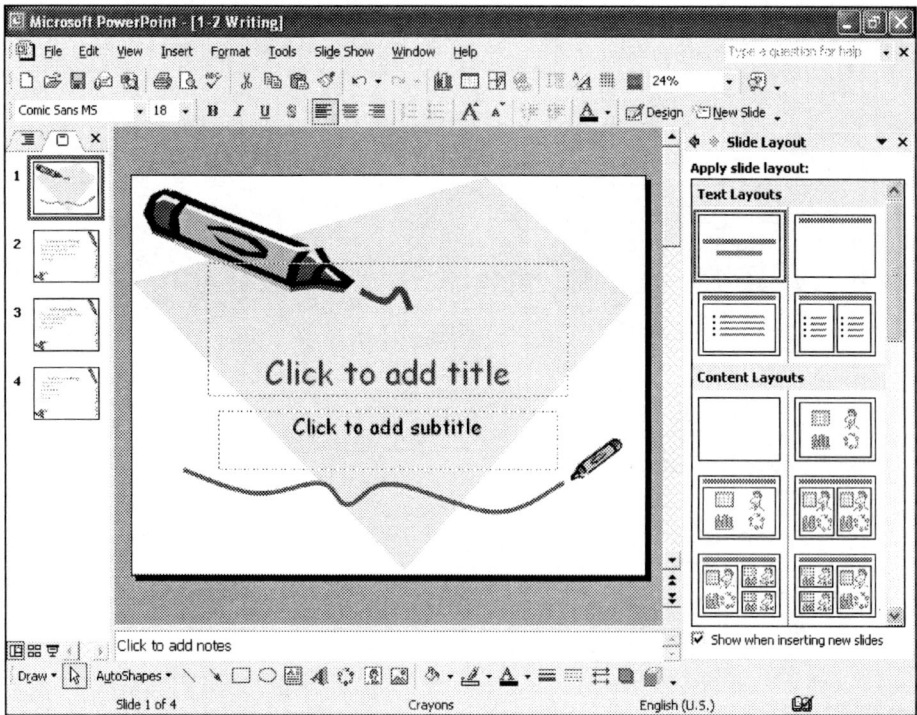

*A blank slide appears immediately. Its number within the presentation appears on the status bar. The **Slide Layout** task pane opens. The slide layout applied to a new slide created in this way is the **Title and Text** layout (from the **Text Layouts** category); if you create a slide at the beginning of the presentation, the **Title Slide** layout is applied.*

* If you wish to use a different slide layout, apply a new layout to the slide.

> *By using the **Slide Layout** task pane, you can choose a layout and create the new slide with one action. To do this, point to the required layout on the task pane, open the list by clicking the arrow that appears on the right and choose the **Insert New Slide** option.*

> *If the insertion point is in the slide body text, you can create a new slide simply by pressing* [Ctrl] [↵] *; PowerPoint creates a new slide, using the same layout as the current slide (unless you create it from a title slide, in which case it creates a "Text and Title" slide).*

5 • Copying/moving slides

* If you are working on several slides, activate the **Slides** tab in Normal view or use Slide Sorter view.

Using the Office Clipboard

With this technique, you can move or copy slides anywhere in the active presentation but also in another presentation or even into another Office application.

* If necessary, display the task pane with **View - Task Pane** then click the ▾ button and choose the **Clipboard** option.

This task pane displays a preview of all the items currently in the Office Clipboard.

* Select the slide(s) concerned.

* To move the slide(s), use:

   Edit - Cut or or ⌈Ctrl⌋ **X**

* To copy the slide(s), use:

   Edit - Copy or or ⌈Ctrl⌋ **C**

   The selection is transferred into the Office Clipboard.

* If necessary, open the presentation into which you wish to paste the copied slide(s) and click the slide after which the pasted slide(s) should appear.

* Click the item you want to paste in the **Clipboard** task pane.

If you copy or move several slides at once into the clipboard, only the first of these appears.

📄 *You can use the Office Clipboard in all the Microsoft Office applications. Simply open the **Clipboard** task pane in the application concerned.*

The 📋 Paste All *button on the **Clipboard** task pane will paste in all the items contained in the Office Clipboard simultaneously (one beneath the other).*

*The Office Clipboard empties itself when you close all the Microsoft Office applications. If you wish to remove any particular item, point to that item on the **Clipboard** task pane, click the arrow that appears on its right and choose the **Delete** option. If you want to empty the Office Clipboard manually, click the* 🗙 Clear All *button on the **Clipboard** task pane.*

By dragging

* Select the slide(s) you wish to move or copy.

* To move a selection, drag it into its new position. To copy a selection, hold down the ⌷Ctrl⌷ key and drag it into its new position.

📄 *This technique can be used to move both text and objects.*

📑6 ▪ Inserting slides from another presentation

* Activate the slide which should appear before the slides you are importing from another presentation.

* **Insert - Slides from Files**

* Using the **Browse** button, select the presentation that contains the slide(s) you want to insert.

PRESENTATIONS AND SLIDES
Lesson 1.2: Slides

PowerPoint examines the selected presentation and shows a preview of its slides in the dialog box.

- Choose how you want that preview to appear:

  to see thumbnails of the slides in the chosen presentation.

  to see only the slide titles.

- Select and insert the required slides:

  - if you want to insert all the slides, click the **Insert All** button.

  - if you want to insert a selection of adjacent slides, click each slide required then click the **Insert** button.

  The chosen slides are inserted into the active presentation and take on the characteristics of the current template.

- Click the **Close** button to close the **Slide Finder** dialog box.

📖7 ▪ Deleting one or more slides

▪ Select the slide(s) you want to delete.

▪ **Edit - Delete Slide**
or
Edit - Clear or ⬚Del⬚

📖8 ▪ Numbering slides

You can number slides automatically; the slide numbers appear in the bottom right corner of each slide.

▪ In Normal view, select the slides you wish to number (if you wish to number only certain slides).

▪ **Insert - Slide Number**

*The **Header and Footer** dialog box opens.*

▪ Tick the **Slide number** check box.

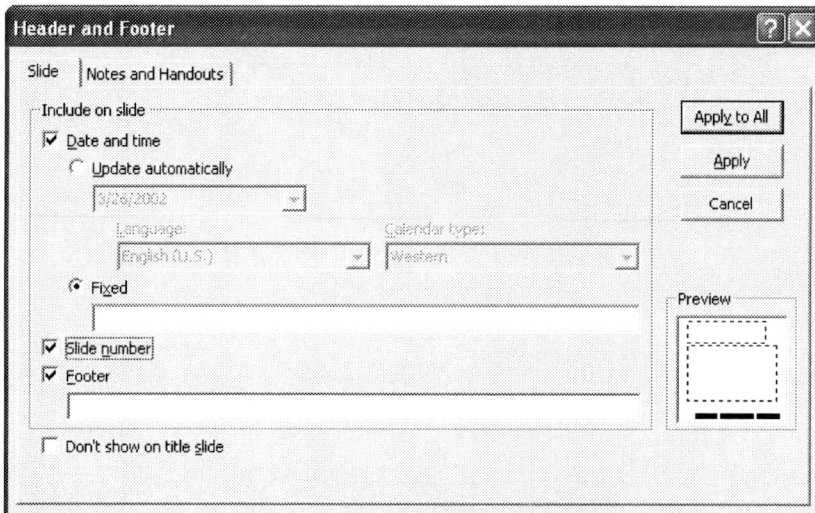

PRESENTATIONS AND SLIDES
Lesson 1.2: Slides

* To apply the slide numbers to only the selected slides, click the **Apply** button. To apply slide numbers to the whole presentation, including the slide master, click the **Apply to All** button.

* If you wish to change where the slide numbering starts, use the **File - Page Setup** command.

* In the **Number slides from** box, enter the slide from which slide numbering should start.

* Click **OK**.

To modify the position and appearance of slide numbers, work on the corresponding area on the slide master.

Below you can see **Practice Exercise** 1.2. This exercise is made up of 8 steps. If you do not know how to do one of the steps, go back to the title that corresponds to that particular lesson. When you have finished, you can check your work by reading the **Solution** that follows.

Steps that are likely to be tested during the MOUS exam are marked with this symbol: 🔲. However, it is a good idea to complete the whole exercise to ensure you have understood everything covered in the lesson.

☞ Practice Exercise 1.2

*To work on exercise 1.2, you should open the **1-2 Writing.ppt** presentation, which is in the **MOUS PowerPoint 2002** folder.*

1. Scroll through all the slides one by one then return to the first slide.

2. Select all the slides in the presentation.

🔲 3. Change the layout of all the slides in the presentation, choosing to apply a **Title and Text** layout.

🔲 4. Add a slide at the beginning of the presentation, keeping the Title Slide layout. Enter **Westport Writer's Workshop** as the title and **Overview** as the subtitle.

🔲 5. Switch the positions of slides **2** and **3**.

🔲 6. At the end of the current presentation, insert all the slides from the **1-2 Workshop.ppt** presentation.

🔲 7. Delete slides **5** and **6**.

PRESENTATIONS AND SLIDES
Exercise 1.2: Slides

8. Number all the slides except the first one.
   Finish by saving and closing the **1-2 Writing** presentation.

If you want to put what you have learnt into practice on a real document, you can work on summary exercise 1 for the PRESENTATIONS AND SLIDES section, that you can find at the end of this book.

It is often possible to perform a task in several different ways, but here only the easiest solution is presented. You can go back to the corresponding lesson if you want to see other techniques you could use.

Solution to Exercise 1.2

1. To scroll through all the slides one by one, press the [PgDn] key twice. To return to the first slide, press the [Home] key.

2. To select all the slides in the presentation, make sure the **Slides** tab is active then use [Ctrl] **A**.

3. To change the layout of all the slides in the presentation, applying a Title and Text layout, start by selecting all the slides, if necessary, by clicking the **Slides** tab then using [Ctrl] **A**.

   Use the **Format - Slide Layout** command.

   On the **Slide Layout** task pane, look in the **Text Layouts** section, point to the layout called **Title and Text** (this is the second layout in the first column) and click this layout to apply it.

4. To add a slide at the beginning of the presentation, keeping the Title Slide layout, click above the first slide in the **Slides** tab (a flashing horizontal bar should appear) and click the [New Slide] button.

   Click the **Click to add title** placeholder and type **Westport Writer's Workshop**. Click the **Click to add subtitle** placeholder and type **Overview**.

5. To switch over slides 2 and 3, click slide **2** in the **Slides** tab and drag it beneath slide **3**.

6. To insert all the slides from the 1-2 Workshop.ppt presentation at the end of the current presentation, click the last slide in the presentation.

Use the **Insert - Slides from Files** command.

Click the **Browse** button. Open the **Look in** list and select the drive on which you copied the contents of the CD-ROM supplied with this book. Double-click the **MOUS PowerPoint 2002** folder then double-click the **1-2 Workshop.ppt** presentation.

Click the **Insert All** button then click **Close** to leave the dialog box.

7. To delete slides 5 and 6, select them with a [Shift]-click then press the [Del] key.

8. To number all the slides except the first one, click slide **2**, hold down the [Shift] key and click slide **5**.

Use the **Insert - Slide Number** command. Activate the **Slide number** check box then click the **Apply** button.

To save and close the 1-2 Writing presentation, click the [save] tool button then use the **File - Close** command.

PRESENTATIONS AND SLIDES
Lesson 1.3: Printing

1 ▪ Modifying the printing format of slides

▪ **File - Page Setup**

▪ To change the size used when printing the slides, choose the required option in the **Slides sized for** list.

As soon as you make your choice, PowerPoint automatically sets values in the **Height** *and* **Width** *boxes to fill the printing area for the active printer.*

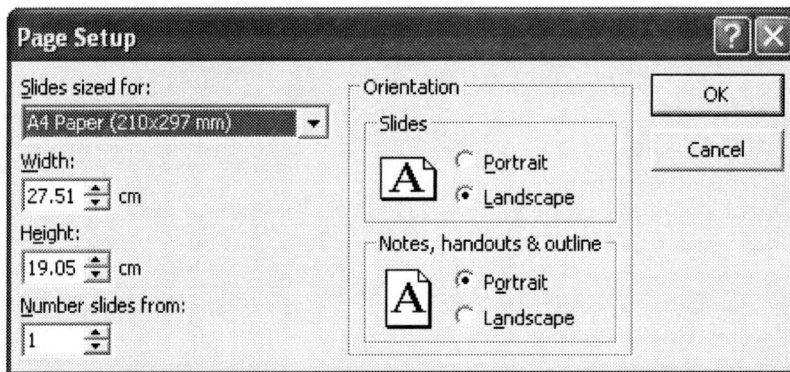

The **Overhead** *choice that is also in the list does not change the size but prints your slides as overhead transparencies.*

▪ Under **Slides**, choose the orientation of the paper for printing slides.

▪ Under **Notes, handouts & outline**, choose the slide orientation for printing handouts, outlines and so on.

▪ Click **OK**.

2 ▪ Previewing slides before printing them

▪ **File - Print Preview** or

※ In the **Print What** list, choose the format in which you want to display the print preview:

Slides	Each slide is printed on one page and will take up as much space as possible on that page.
Handouts (1 to **9 slides per page)**	Displays the specified number of slides on each page, in varying layouts.
Notes Pages	Prints notes (one slide per page, followed by its notes).
Outline View	Prints just the outline of the presentation.

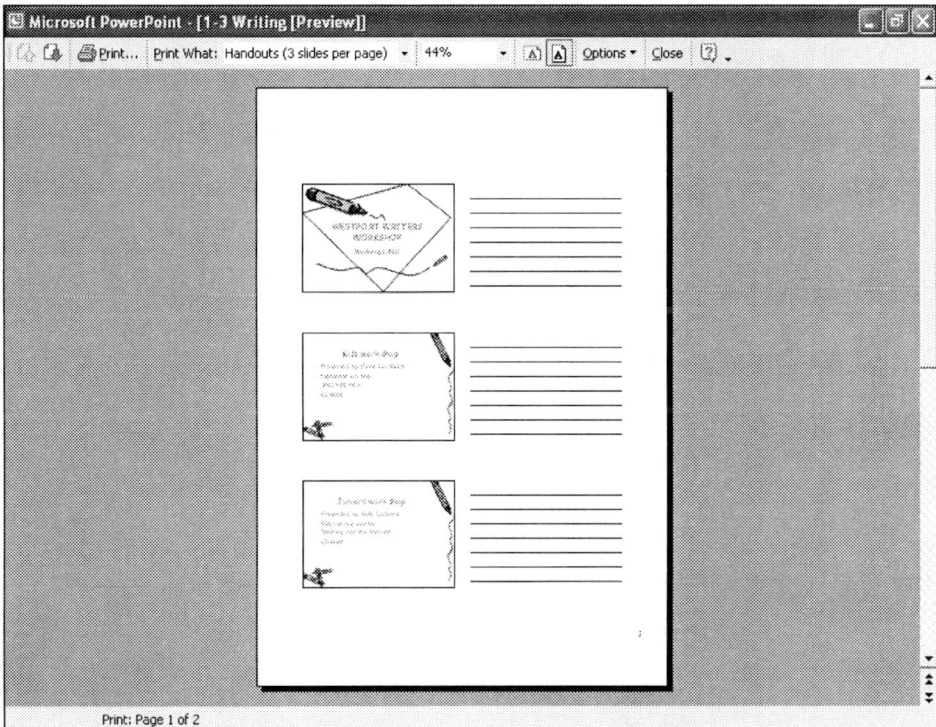

* Use the tool buttons to work on the preview:

* To draw a border around the slides when they print, open the list on the **Options** button and activate the **Frame slides** option.

* If you are printing 4, 6 or 9 slides per page and you wish to modify the way the slides are laid out on the page, open the list on the **Options** button and point to the **Printing Order** option, then choose **Horizontal** (arranged in rows) or **Vertical** (arranged in columns).

* To make what is being printed fill as much space on the page as possible, activate the **Scale to Fit Paper** option, in the **Options** list.

* Click **Close** to leave the print preview.

3 ▪ Creating headers and footers

Creating footers for slides printed in Slides format

This technique is used to create footers on slides that will be printed in Slides format (which prints one slide per page).

* If necessary, select the slides to which you want to apply a footer. If you are applying it to all the slides and the master, you do not have to select anything.

* In the print preview window, open the **Options** list and choose **Header and Footer**; if you are in the presentation window, use **View - Header and Footer** or show the slide master.

▪ If necessary, click the **Slide** tab then use these options:

Update automatically	to print the current date at the bottom left of each side, in the specified **Language**.
Fixed	to print a date or a text (that you can enter in the accompanying text box) at the bottom left of each slide.
Slide number	to print the number of the slide at the bottom right of each slide.
Footer	activate this option and enter a text in the accompanying text box; this prints at the bottom centre of each slide.

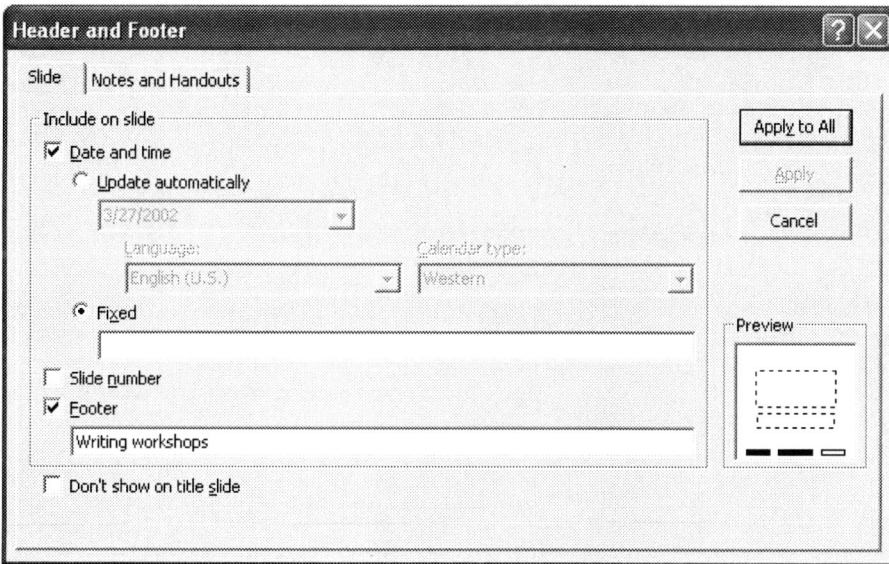

*When you activate each option, the **Preview** box displays the area concerned in black.*

▪ Activate the **Don't show on title slide** option if you do not want to apply the footer to any slides with a Title Slide layout.

* Click the **Apply** button to add the footer to only the selected slides or click **Apply to All** to add the footer to all the slides in the presentation and the slide master.

Creating headers/footers for printing handouts, notes or outlines

Use this technique to create headers or footers on each page when you print handouts (1 to 9 slides per page), notes pages or outlines.

* In the print preview window, open the **Options** list and choose **Header and Footer**; if you are in the presentation window, use **View - Header and Footer** or show the slide master.

* Click the **Notes and Handouts** tab.

* Set the following options:

Update automatically	to print the current date at the top right of each page, in the specified **Language**.
Fixed	to print a date or a text (that you can enter in the accompanying text box) at the top right of each page.
Header	to print the text entered in the accompanying text box at the top left of each page.
Page number	to print the number of the slide at the bottom right of each page.
Footer	activate this option and enter a text in the accompanying text box; this prints at the bottom left of each page.

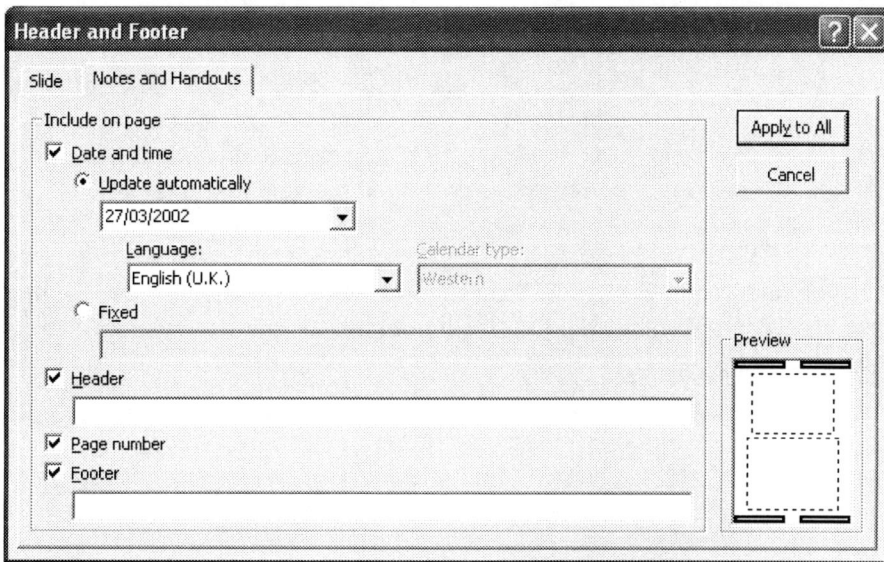

* Click the **Apply to All** button.

4 • Printing a presentation

* Select the slides you want to print. If you are printing them all, you do not need to make a selection.

* **File - Print** or [Ctrl] **P**

   *You can also print by clicking the **Print** button on the print preview window.*

* In the **Print range** frame, specify which slides you want to print:

All	To print all the slides in the presentation.
Current slide	To print the slide in which the insertion point is currently positioned.
Selection	To print previously selected slides.

Slides   To print individual slides. In the text box, enter the numbers of the slides concerned separated by commas, or for a group of consecutive slides, enter the first number, a dash then the last number.

* In the **Copies** frame, give the **Number of copies** you wish to print.

* If you are printing multiple copies, you can if necessary activate the **Collate** option. PowerPoint then prints a full copy of the entire document before starting on the next one.

* In the **Print what** list, choose what you wish to print: **Slides**, **Handouts** (to print several slides on a single page), **Notes Pages** or **Outline View**.

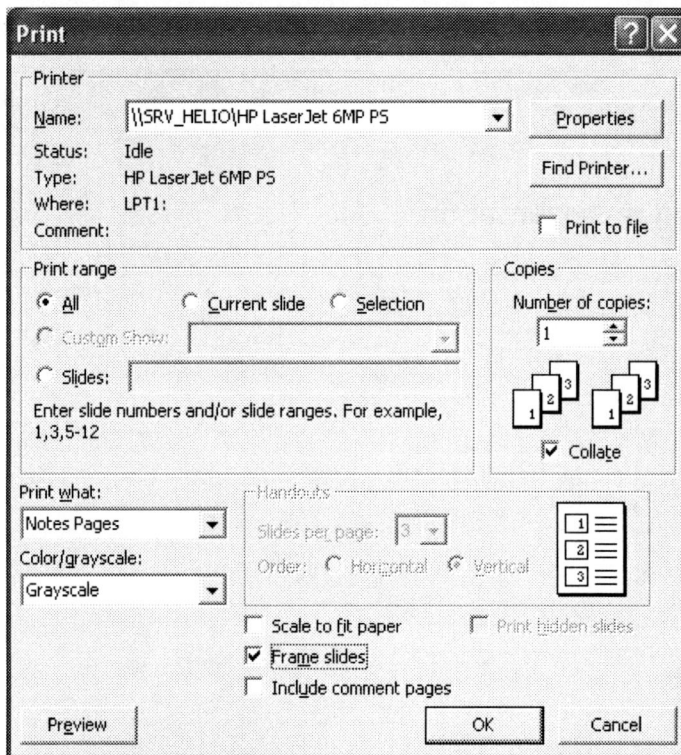

✳ If you chose to print **Handouts** (in the **Print what** list), go to the **Handouts** frame and choose the number of **Slides per page**.

✳ In the **Color/grayscale** list, specify if you want to print in **Color**, in **Grayscale** or in **Pure Black and White** (PowerPoint transforms all grayscales into black or white).

✳ Activate the **Scale to fit paper** option to adjust the size of the slide's image so it fills the page of paper.

✳ If you wish to **Frame slides** with a border, activate the corresponding option.

✳ Activate the **Include comment pages** option to print a page containing all the comments in the presentation.

✳ If the presentation contains hidden slides, print them by activating the **Print hidden slides** option.

*You will also find all of these options in the **Options** list in the print preview window.*

✳ Click the **Preview** button to see a preview before you print or start printing by clicking **OK**.

You can customise printing notes pages or handouts from the respective masters. In the master you can create and/or modify headers and footers, format the background and so on. The changes you make appear on the print preview and in the printed result.

*The tool button on the **Standard** toolbar will print the presentation with the current print options, without going through the **Print** dialog box.*

PRESENTATIONS AND SLIDES
Exercise 1.3: Printing

Below you can see **Practice Exercise** 1.3. This exercise is made up of 4 steps. If you do not know how to do one of the steps, go back to the title that corresponds to that particular lesson. When you have finished, you can check your work by reading the **Solution** that follows.

Steps that are likely to be tested during the MOUS exam are marked with this symbol: ⊞. However, it is a good idea to complete the whole exercise to ensure you have understood everything covered in the lesson.

☞ **Practice Exercise 1.3**

*To work on exercise 1.3, you should open the **1-3 Writing.ppt** presentation in the **MOUS PowerPoint 2002** folder.*

1. Apply an **A4 Paper** format for printing the slides.

⊞ 2. Display the presentation in the print preview, choosing to see three handouts per page. Close the print preview.

⊞ 3. Create the following headers and footers:

   - at the bottom centre of each individual slide, display the text **Writing workshops**,

   - at the top right, when printing handouts, notes pages or outlines, the current date should appear.

⊞ 4. Print the notes pages of all the slides, applying a frame to the slides. Save and close the **1-3 Writing** presentation.

If you want to put what you have learnt into practice on a real document, you can work on summary exercise 1 for the PRESENTATIONS AND SLIDES section, that you can find at the end of this book.

It is often possible to perform a task in several different ways, but here only the easiest solution is presented. You can go back to the corresponding lesson if you want to see other techniques you could use.

Solution to Exercise 1.3

1. To apply an A4 Paper format for printing the slides in the 1-3 Writing presentation, use the **File - Page Setup** command.
In the **Slides sized for** list, choose **A4 Paper (210x297 mm)** format. Click **OK**.

2. To preview the presentation, click the ![icon] tool button.

   To show three handouts per page, open the **Print What** list on the toolbar and choose the **Handouts (3 slides per page)** option.

   To leave the print preview, click the **Close** button on its toolbar.

3. To create a footer at the bottom centre of each slide that displays the text "Writing workshops", start by using the **View - Header and Footer** command. Click the **Slide** tab then click the **Footer** box and type **Writing workshops**.

   To print the current date at the top right of handouts, notes pages or outlines, click the **Notes and Handouts** tab then activate the **Update automatically** option. Click the **Apply to All** button.

4. To print the presentation's notes pages, use **File - Print** and in the **Print range** frame, specify that you want to print **All** the slides.
In the **Print what** list, select the **Notes Pages** option. Activate the **Frame slides** option. Click **OK** to start printing.

   To finish, save the **1-3 Writing** presentation with the ![icon] tool button and close it with **File - Close**.

PRESENTATIONS AND SLIDES
Exercise 1.3: Printing

WORKING WITH TEXT
Lesson 2.1: Entering and editing text

WORKING WITH TEXT
Lesson 2.1: Entering and editing text

1 ▪ Entering text

Entering a slide's title and subtitle

▪ Click in the placeholder where you can see the text **Click to add title** or **Click to add subtitle**.

The prompt disappears and in its place you can see a frame with a hatched border. A vertical bar, called the insertion point, flashes inside that frame.

▪ Type your title or subtitle text.

▪ If necessary, confirm your text with Esc.

While the insertion point is in the title, you can press Ctrl ↵ to go to the next placeholder; if the insertion point is in the subtitle or body text and you press Ctrl ↵, you create a new slide.

Entering the body text of a slide

▪ Click the body text placeholder, where you can see the text **Click to add text** or, if the insertion point is in the title, you can use Ctrl ↵ to go to the text placeholder.

The main area of the slide is enclosed within a hatched border. The insertion point appears in this border, preceded by a bullet.

* Type the contents of a bulleted list, keeping in mind the following points:

  - Enter the text without worrying about the end of lines, and only press ⏎ when you want to go to the next bullet point.

  - Use [Ctrl][⇆] to insert a tab stop at the beginning of a line or [⇆] to insert one anywhere else in the line.

  - Press [Shift]⏎ to create empty lines.

  Each paragraph of text is preceded by a bullet.

* You can add hierarchical levels to your list: to descend by one paragraph level, place the insertion point at the beginning of the line and press [⇆] or to move up one paragraph level, place the insertion point at the beginning of the line and press [Shift][⇆].

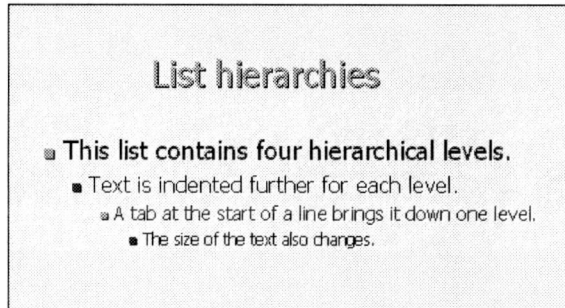

List hierarchies

- This list contains four hierarchical levels.
  - Text is indented further for each level.
    - A tab at the start of a line brings it down one level.
      - The size of the text also changes.

Depending on the level you are in, the size of the characters and the bullet point symbols change. You will also notice that the texts are indented in relation to each other.

* If you wish, finish typing by pressing [Esc] or press [Ctrl]⏎ to create a new slide.

📄 *Any text that appears in the title placeholder and in the body text placeholder belongs to the presentation's outline. PowerPoint can use 6 outline levels, the title plus 5 levels within the body text.*

Entering text in the Outline tab

* In Normal view, click [icon] to activate the **Outline** tab.

  *The names of the tabs now appear as text labels: **Outline** and **Slides**.*

* To enter text in each slide:

  - Click to the right of the slide icon.

  - Enter the title then press [Ctrl↵] to start typing the contents of the bulleted list or press [↵] to create a new slide.

  - Type your bulleted list of text, following the same rules as for entering directly into the slide (press [↵] to go to a new line or [Ctrl↵] to create a new slide).

As you type, some words might appear underlined by a red wavy line.
PowerPoint 2002 has detected these words automatically as being misspelled or unknown in the dictionaries that it uses.

* To display the **Outlining** toolbar, use the **View - Toolbars - Outlining** command.

  The toolbar appears along the left side of the window.

* You can add hierarchical levels to your list: to descend by one paragraph level, place the insertion point at the beginning of the line and press [➡] or click the [➡] tool button, or to move up one paragraph level, place the insertion point at the beginning of the line and press [Shift➡] or click the [⬅] tool button.

* To return to the **Slides** tab, click its name.

Entering notes

* In Normal view, click in the **Click to add notes** area (the notes pane) or activate Notes Page view with **View - Notes Page**.
* If you are in Notes Page view, adjust the zoom level if necessary, then click the **Click to add notes** area.
* Type the notes without worrying about the ends of the lines.

By default, there are no bullets in the notes page paragraphs.

*By default, as you enter text into a placeholder, the text is modified so it remains entirely visible within the placeholder area. This is the text AutoFit feature. To manage this option, type your text and click the ⬍ button, which will appear once PowerPoint is obliged to resize the text in the placeholder. To keep your original text size, you can choose to **Split Text Between Two Slides**, to **Continue on a New Slide** or to **Change to Two-Column Layout** (these options do not appear in a title placeholder). To turn off text AutoFit temporarily, choose to **Stop Fitting Text to This Placeholder**. PowerPoint will no longer resize any spillover text and text AutoFit will be turned off on this placeholder for the rest of the current PowerPoint session.*

To place a tab stop at the beginning of a line, press the ⭾ key.

▣2 ▪ Correcting a misspelled word

By default, PowerPoint checks your spelling as you type. When you type a word incorrectly and PowerPoint does not recognise the spelling, the word is underlined with a wavy red line. If the word is in the AutoCorrect list, it is corrected automatically.

▪ To correct a misspelled word, underlined in red, right-click it.

When you right-click the word, a shortcut menu appears.

▪ Depending on the options shown, click:

One of the suggested corrections   to replace the underlined word with the corrected word.

Ignore All   to ignore this word each time it appears during this work session.

Add to Dictionary   to add the underlined word to the custom dictionary, so that PowerPoint will recognise it in the future.

*Spelling mistakes appear underlined only if, in the **Options** dialog box (**Tools - Options - Spelling and Style** tab), the **Check spelling as you type** option is active and the **Hide spelling errors in this document** option is inactive.*

*Some mistakes may be corrected automatically, perhaps without you even realising! This occurs thanks to PowerPoint's AutoCorrect feature (**Tools - AutoCorrect Options - AutoCorrect** tab). In this dialog box, you can add further AutoCorrect entries: add the word you frequently misspell (or an abbreviation you wish to replace with text) in the **Replace** box, type the replacement word or text in the **With** box and click the **Add** button to add the new entry.*

3 ▪ Moving the insertion point in text

- Click the required place, or use the following keys, whatever the active pane:

→/←	next/previous character.
Ctrl → / Ctrl ←	next/previous word.
Home / End	beginning/end of the line.
↓/↑	next/previous line.
Ctrl ↓ / Ctrl ↑	beginning of the next/previous paragraph.
Ctrl Home / Ctrl End	beginning/end of the text in that placeholder.

4 ▪ Editing text in a slide

- Display the slide whose text you wish to modify.
- Click in the text item you want to edit.
- Make your changes, keeping the following points in mind:

  - To add characters, place the insertion point where they are to appear and type (Insert mode is the only editing mode you can use).

  - To delete a character, press Del if the insertion point is before the character or ← if it is after the character.

  - To delete a word, use Ctrl Del if the word is after the insertion point or Ctrl ← if the insertion point is after the word.

  - Delete a group of characters by selecting them and pressing Del.

  - To replace a group of characters, select them and type the new text.

5 ▪ Selecting text

▪ Wherever the insertion point happens to be, to select:

A word   double-click it.

A paragraph   triple-click it.

A group of characters   drag over the characters you want to select or click in front of the first character, point to just after the last one, hold down the [Shift] key and click.

All the text in the current placeholder   use **Edit - Select All** or [Ctrl] **A**.

> To select characters using the keyboard, hold down the [Shift] key and use the arrow keys.

6 ▪ Inserting an outline file into a presentation

An outline file can contain text created in PowerPoint or in other applications; different types of text file are supported, such as *.DOC, *.RTF or *.TXT.

▪ Activate the slide that should precede the new slides that will be created when you insert the outline.

▪ **Insert - Slides from Outline**

▪ Activate the folder that contains the outline you want to insert.

WORKING WITH TEXT
Lesson 2.1: Entering and editing text

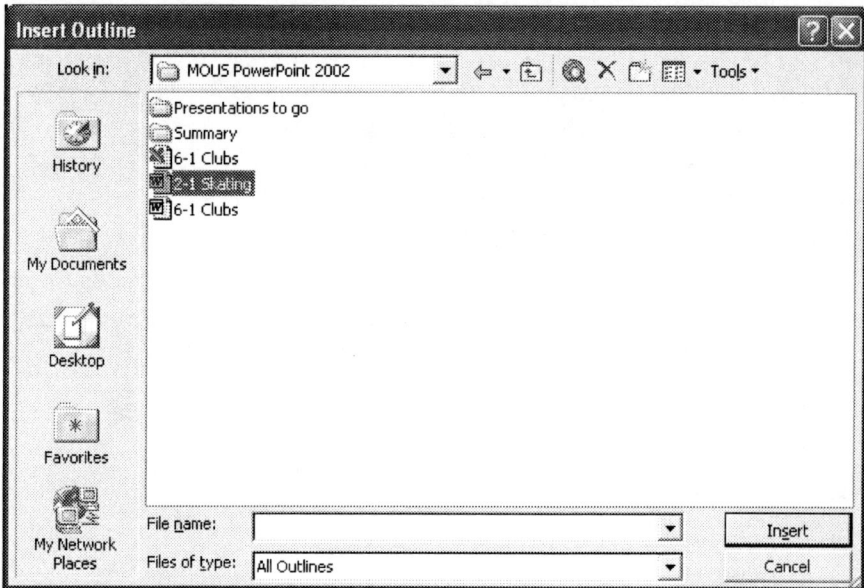

» Double-click the name of the outline file concerned.

*PowerPoint may ask you to install an extra converter. If this occurs, click **Yes** on the dialog box and follow the instructions.*

PowerPoint creates as many slides as there are texts in Heading 1 style, and places the rest of the text in different levels of bulleted lists.

7 ▪ Checking the spelling in a presentation

» Place the insertion point where you want to start the spelling check.

» **Tools - Spelling** or or F7

*PowerPoint goes through all the words and checks whether they are present in its dictionary or the custom dictionary. If an unknown word is found it appears in the **Not in Dictionary** box. The word is also highlighted in the slide.*

» If the word is misspelled:

- if the correct spelling is present in the **Suggestions** list, double-click it.

- if none of the suggestions is appropriate, correct the word in the **Change to** box and click **Change** or **Change All**.

» If the spelling is correct but the word is not in the dictionary, click:

Ignore	to continue the check without correcting the word.
Ignore All	the spelling check continues, and does not stop at that word for the rest of the work session.
Add	the word is added to your custom dictionary, whose name you can see in the **Add words to** box, and the spelling check continues.

* When the spelling check is finished click **OK**.

> *To define the spelling check options, use **Tools - Options** and click the **Spelling and Style** tab. Activate the **Always suggest corrections** option if you want PowerPoint to display a list of suggested corrections; choose whether or not PowerPoint should **Ignore words in UPPERCASE** or **Ignore words with numbers** (these can be useful for checking certain types of text, such as addresses).*
>
> *The **Style Options** button on the **Options** dialog box (**Spelling and Style** tab) contains options concerning the correction of styles, including punctuation errors, text readability and so on.*

8 ▪ Finding/replacing text

You do not need to put the insertion point in a particular place, as PowerPoint will search the whole presentation.

Finding text

* **Edit - Find** or $\boxed{\text{Ctrl}}$ **F**
* Type the text you are looking for in the **Find what** box.
* Activate the following options if necessary:

Match case	to find the word you are looking for with the same combination of upper and lower case letters as entered in the **Find what** box. PowerPoint will look for "hour" (for example), but may also find "Hour" and "HOUR". If you only want to find "hour" you should activate **Match case**.
Find whole words only	if the word you are looking for is a whole word. For example, for the word "hour", if **Find whole words only** is deactivated PowerPoint may find "hour", but also "hours" or "hourly", but if **Find whole words only** is active PowerPoint will find only find the word "hour".

Find

Find what:
rollerblading

☐ Match case
☐ Find whole words only

Find Next

Close

Replace...

⁑ Start searching by clicking **Find Next**.

Wherever the insertion point happens to be in the presentation, the first occurrence of the word is found.

⁑ Click **Find Next** to continue searching. To stop the search, click **Close**.

📄 *The **Replace** button in the **Find** dialog box opens the **Replace** dialog box.*

🔍 *When the **Find** dialog box is closed, you can restart the last search by pressing* [Shift] [F4].

Replacing text

⁑ **Edit - Replace** or [Ctrl] **H**

⁑ Type the text you want to find, which is the text you want to replace, in the **Find what** box.

⁑ Type the replacement text in the **Replace with** box.

Replace

Find what:
Green Park

Replace with:
Lang Park

☑ Match case
☐ Find whole words only

Find Next

Close

Replace

Replace All

WORKING WITH TEXT
Lesson 2.1: Entering and editing text

- Indicate the search and replace criteria (which are the same as those used in the **Find** dialog box).

- Choose to replace all the text without being asked for confirmation (click **Replace All**) or to replace word by word (using the **Find Next** and **Replace** buttons).

- When the replacement is finished, click **OK**.

- Close the replacement dialog box by clicking **Close**.

9 ▪ Saving a presentation as an outline file

This saves the outline of a presentation. This file, whose name does not appear on the title bar, can be read by PowerPoint, but also by other applications, such as Microsoft Word.

- **File - Save As**

- Open the **Save as type** list and choose **Outline/RTF**.

- If necessary, enter a new **File name**.

* Using the **Save in** list or the **Places Bar**, choose where you wish to store this file.

* Click the **Save** button.

> *To create a presentation from an outline file, simply open the file with the **File - Open** command. Open the **Files of type** list and choose the **All Outlines** option to see only outline files. Activate the folder that contains the outline file and double-click the file name.*

Below you can see **Practice Exercise** 2.1. This exercise is made up of 9 steps. If you do not know how to do one of the steps, go back to the title that corresponds to that particular lesson. When you have finished, you can check your work by reading the **Solution** that follows.

Steps that are likely to be tested during the MOUS exam are marked with this symbol: ⊞. However, it is a good idea to complete the whole exercise to ensure you have understood everything covered in the lesson.

☞ **Practice Exercise 2.1**

*To work on exercise 2.1 you will need to open the **2-1 Skating.ppt** presentation in the **MOUS PowerPoint 2002** folder.*

⊞ 1. On the first slide, enter the following text: **Rollerbladers** as the title, **Inline Skating Association** as the first line of the subtitle and **A sport for all** as the second line of the subtitle. Next, create a second slide and enter the following text:

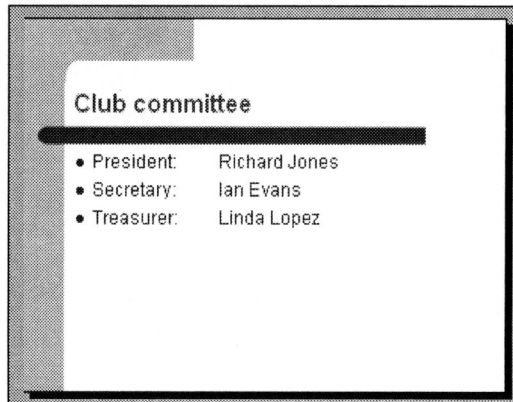

Club committee

- President: Richard Jones
- Secretary: Ian Evans
- Treasurer: Linda Lopez

Create a third slide and activate the Outline tab then enter the text below:

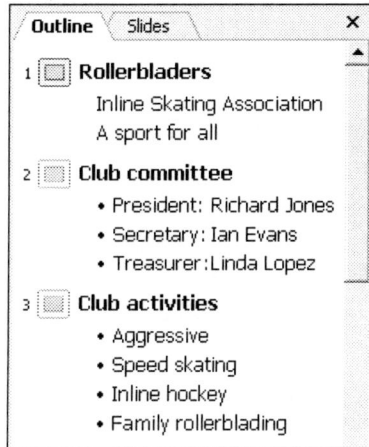

```
┌─────────────────────────────────────┐
│ Outline    Slides              ✕     │
│                                   ▲  │
│  1 □  Rollerbladers                  │
│        Inline Skating Association    │
│        A sport for all               │
│                                      │
│  2 ▥  Club committee                 │
│        • President: Richard Jones    │
│        • Secretary: Ian Evans        │
│        • Treasurer: Linda Lopez      │
│                                      │
│  3 ▥  Club activities                │
│        • Aggressive                  │
│        • Speed skating               │
│        • Inline hockey               │
│        • Family rollerblading        │
└─────────────────────────────────────┘
```

On this third slide enter a note: **A new aggressive skateing ramp will be available by the end of the spring**. You should take care to keep the spelling mistake in the word "skateing". To finish, return to the **Slides** tab.

2. Use PowerPoint's automatic spelling check features to ignore the unknown word "Rollerbladers" on slide 1 and to correct the spelling mistake in "skateing" in the notes pane on slide 3.

3. Move the insertion point to the first slide, at the end of the text **A sport for all**.

4. Change the text **A sport for all** to **A great sport for all**.

5. Select the word **Association** on the title slide and change it to **Club**.

6. Insert the outline file called **2-1 Skating.doc**, from the **MOUS PowerPoint 2002** folder, after the last slide in the active presentation.

7. Check and correct the spelling in the whole presentation.

8. Replace each occurrence of the phrase **Green Park** by the phrase **Lang Park**, matching the character case.

▦ 9. Save the active presentation into the **MOUS PowerPoint 2002** folder as an outline file, that you can name **2-1 Skating club**.
Save and close the active file.

If you want to put what you have learnt into practice on a real document, you can work on summary exercise 2 for the WORKING WITH TEXT section, that you can find at the end of this book.

It is often possible to perform a task in several different ways, but here only the easiest solution is presented. You can go back to the corresponding lesson if you want to see other techniques you could use.

Solution to Exercise 2.1

1. To enter the title and subtitles of the first slide, click the **Click to add title** placeholder and enter **Rollerbladers**, press ⌨Ctrl⌨ then enter **Inline Skating Association**, press ⌨ and enter **A sport for all**.

   Press ⌨Ctrl⌨ to create a new slide.

   Click the **Click to add title** placeholder and enter **Club committee**. Press ⌨Ctrl⌨ and type **President:** ⌨ **Richard Jones** ⌨ **Secretary:** ⌨ **Ian Evans** ⌨ **Treasurer:** ⌨ **Linda Lopez**.

   Press ⌨Ctrl⌨ to create the third slide and click the ⌨ tab to activate the **Outline** tab. Click to the right of the third slide's icon and type **Club activities** ⌨Ctrl⌨ **Aggressive** ⌨ **Speed skating** ⌨ **Inline hockey** ⌨ **Family rollerblading**

   To enter the note specified in the exercise, in slide 3, click in the Notes pane (where the **Click to add notes** text appears) and type **A new aggressive skateing ramp will be available by the end of the spring** (complete with spelling mistake).

   To return to the **Slides** tab, click this tab.

2. To ignore the spelling error indicated by PowerPoint's automatic spelling checker on the word "Rollerbladers", activate slide 1, right-click that word and choose **Ignore All**. To correct the spelling mistake in "skateing", go to slide 3, right-click the word **skateing** in the notes pane and choose the **skating** correction.

3. To move the insertion point to the first slide, at the end of the text "A sport for all", click the picture of the first slide in the **Slides** tab then in the slide pane, click the text **A sport for all**. Press the [End] key to place the insertion point at the end of the line.

4. Change the text "A sport for all" to "A great sport for all" by clicking after the letter **A** at the start of the sentence and typing [Space] **great**.

5. To select the word "Association" on the title slide in order to change it to "Club", double-click the word **Association** on the first slide and type **Club**.

6. To insert the 2-1 Skating.doc outline file from the MOUS PowerPoint 2002 folder, click the third slide icon on the **Slides** tab to go to the last slide.
Activate **Insert - Slides from Outline**.
If necessary, activate the **MOUS PowerPoint 2002** folder then double-click the **2-1 Skating.doc** file.

   If PowerPoint asks you to install a component, click **Yes** and follow the instructions (you may need the application CD-ROM).

7. To check the spelling in the whole presentation, press [Ctrl][Home] to move to the beginning of the active presentation then start the spelling check by clicking the [ABC✓] tool button. Replace the word "superviesd" with the word **supervised**, the word "fontain" with **fountain** and the word "frendly" with **friendly**. At the end of the check, click **OK**.

8. To search for the phrase "Green Park" to replace it with the phrase "Lang Park", use the **Edit - Replace** command and type the words **Green Park** in the **Find what** box. Click the **Replace with** box and type **Lang Park**. To respect the uppercase/lowercase characters, tick the **Match case** option.

   Click the **Replace All** button to make all the replacements at once. Click **OK** when PowerPoint tells you that all the replacements have been carried out then click the **Close** button on the **Replace** dialog box.

9. To save the active presentation as an outline file called 2-1 Skating club, use the **File - Save As** command.

Open the **Save in** list and choose the drive onto which you copied the CD-ROM supplied with this book, then open the **MOUS PowerPoint 2002** folder. In the **File name** box, type **2-1 Skating club** then open the **Save as type** list and choose the **Outline/RTF** option. Click the **Save** button to save the outline file.

To close the **2-1 Skating.ppt** file, use **File - Close** and click **Yes** if PowerPoint prompts you to save the file.

WORKING WITH TEXT
Exercise 2.1: Entering and editing text

WORKING WITH TEXT
Lesson 2.2: Formatting text

WORKING WITH TEXT
Lesson 2.2: Formatting text

1 ▪ Modifying character font

▪ Select the placeholder, text object or characters concerned. To change the font used for all paragraphs of a particular level, open the slide master and click the level concerned.

▪ Open the **Font** list box on the **Formatting** toolbar.

The fonts that appear above the double line are those that were used last (PowerPoint lists up to the last six fonts used).

▪ Click the name of the font of your choice. Some fonts display a TT symbol, which indicates they are TrueType fonts managed by Windows (these generally give a more consistent result).

📄 *From the keyboard, you can access the **Font** list using the* Ctrl Shift **F** *shortcut key.*

*You can also modify the font with the **Format - Font** command.*

2 ▪ Replacing a font over an entire presentation

This is a useful technique for replacing one font with another each time it occurs in a presentation, in a single action.

▪ Make sure the insertion point is not in a placeholder.

Format - Replace Fonts

No matter where the insertion point is positioned, PowerPoint will replace the font wherever it occurs in the presentation.

- Open the **Replace** list and choose the font you wish to replace.

Only fonts used in the current presentation figure in this list.

- Open the **With** list and choose the new font.

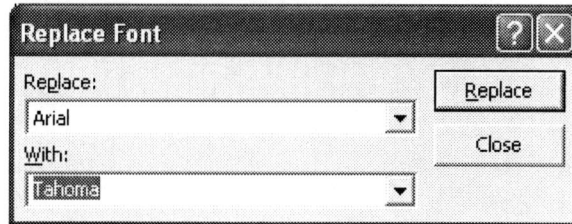

- Click the **Replace** button.

*When PowerPoint has made all its replacements, the **Replace** button becomes unavailable and the font you replaced is changed in the **Replace** list, as it no longer exists in the presentation.*

- Leave the **Replace Font** dialog box by clicking the **Close** button.

3 ▪ Modifying character size

Increasing/decreasing character size

- Select the placeholder or text object or string of characters concerned. If you want to make changes to all the paragraphs of a particular level, go to the slide master and click the level concerned.

- Depending on your requirements, click:

  to apply the next character size up from the one shown in the **Font Size** box (on the **Formatting** toolbar).

  to apply the next size down from that shown in the **Font Size** box.

Choosing a specific size

※ Select the placeholder, text object or string of characters concerned. If you want to make changes to all the paragraphs of a particular level, go to the slide master and click the level concerned.

※ Open the **Font Size** list on the **Formatting** toolbar.

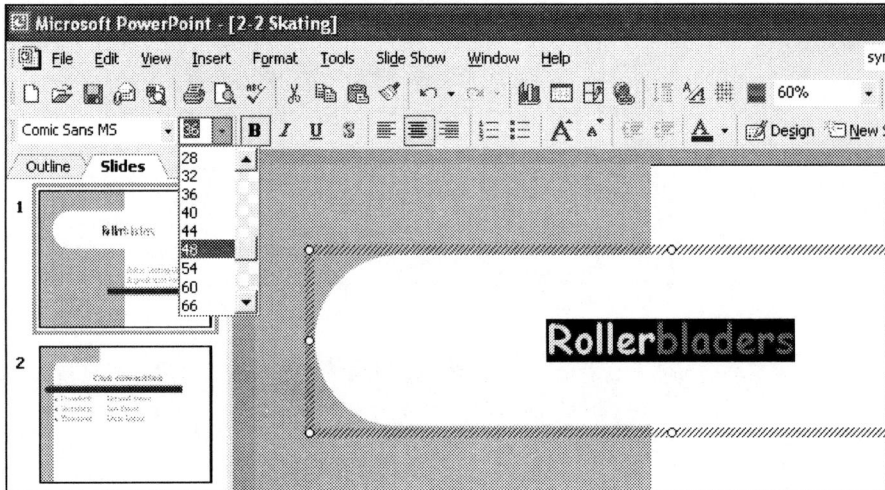

※ Click the required font size or enter your own value in the text box, remembering to press ⏎ to confirm.

📄 *You can access the **Font Size** list with the* Ctrl Shift *P shortcut key.*

*You can also modify font size by using the **Format - Font** command.*

4 ▪ Modifying character formatting

※ Select the placeholder, text object or characters concerned. If you want to make changes to all the paragraphs of a particular level, go to the slide master and click the level concerned.

» Depending on the attribute you want to apply, use one of the following techniques:

	Bold	**Italics**	**Underlining**	**Shadow**
🖱	**B**	*I*	<u>U</u>	S
⌨	Ctrl B	Ctrl I	Ctrl U	

📄 *To deactivate an attribute, either click the same tool button again or repeat the shortcut key.*

» Select the placeholder, text object or characters concerned. If you want to make changes to all the paragraphs of a particular level, go to the slide master and click the level concerned.

» **Format - Font**

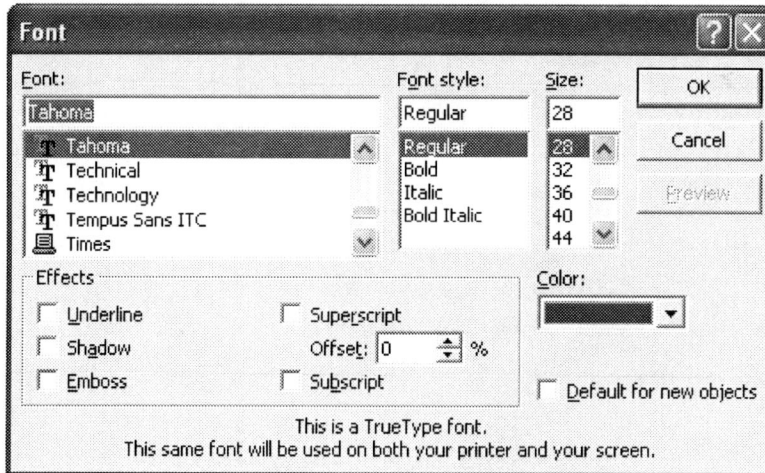

*The **Offset** text box lets you enter a value by which to raise or lower the text in relation to the baseline. A positive value activates the **Superscript** option and a negative value activates **Subscript**.*

» Activate the formatting attributes you want to apply.

* Confirm by clicking **OK**.

> The quickest way to remove all character formatting on selected text is to use the `Ctrl` `Shift` **Z** or `Ctrl` `Space` shortcut keys.

🔖5 ▪ Applying a shadow effect to text

*This action applies a **Shadow** style to all the text in the active placeholder.*

* Select the placeholder or text object concerned. If you wish to modify the entire presentation, go to the slide master and click the placeholder in question.

* Click the ⬛ tool button on the **Drawing** toolbar.

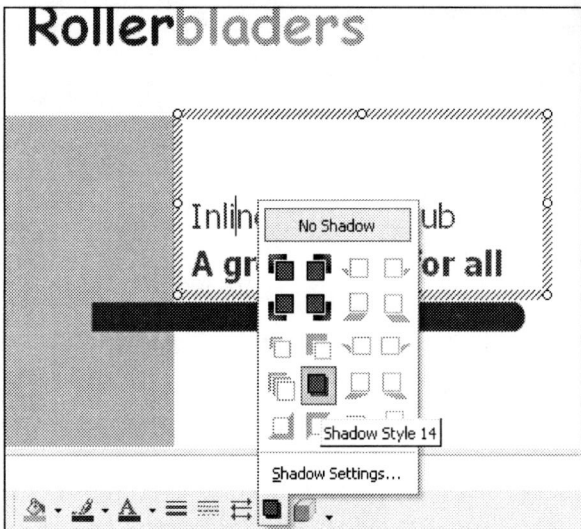

You can see that only five options are not greyed-out; these are the only options you can apply to text. The **No Shadow** option removes any shadows applied to a selected text.

* Click the required type of shadow.
* Click outside the placeholder or text object to finish.

📘6 ▪ Applying a colour to text

▪ Select the placeholder or text object or characters concerned. If you want to make changes to all the paragraphs of a particular level, go to the slide master and click the level concerned.

▪ Open the 🅰️ list on the **Drawing** or **Formatting** toolbar by clicking the arrow on the button.

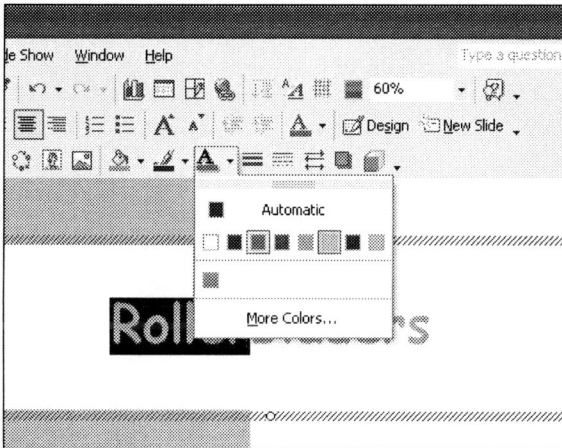

You have the choice of eight basic colours; these vary according to the template used for the slides in the presentation. Recently used custom colours may appear under the row of basic colours. The **More Colors** option lets you access other colours. The **Automatic** option retrieves the default colour.

▪ Click either your choice of colour swatch or one of the options proposed.

▪ If you opt for **More Colors**:

- activate the **Standard** tab and click the colour swatch you require,

or

- activate the **Custom** tab and drag the cross-shaped pointer to choose a colour then drag the slider on the right to change that colour's luminosity (you can even select a different **Color model** if you wish or choose a specific colour by entering its colour values in the appropriate text boxes),

- then confirm with **OK**.

📄 *The last colour chosen is added to the palette of eight basic colours in the* 🅰️ *list and is displayed on the tool button itself.*

*You can also change the colour of text with the **Format - Font** command.*

📄7 ▪ Managing bullets on paragraphs

※ Select the text concerned. If you want to make changes to all the paragraphs of a particular level, go to the slide master and click the level concerned.

Displaying/hiding bullets

※ Click the 📋 tool button.

This tool adds and removes bullets from the current paragraph(s).

📄 *You can also use **Format - Bullets and Numbering - Bulleted** tab and activate the **None** option to remove bulleting.*

Changing the bullet used on a paragraph

※ **Format - Bullets and Numbering - Bulleted** tab

※ Click one of the seven boxes depending on which bullet you wish to use.

※ If necessary, change the **Size** of the bullet, as a **% of text** and/or the **Color** of the bullet.

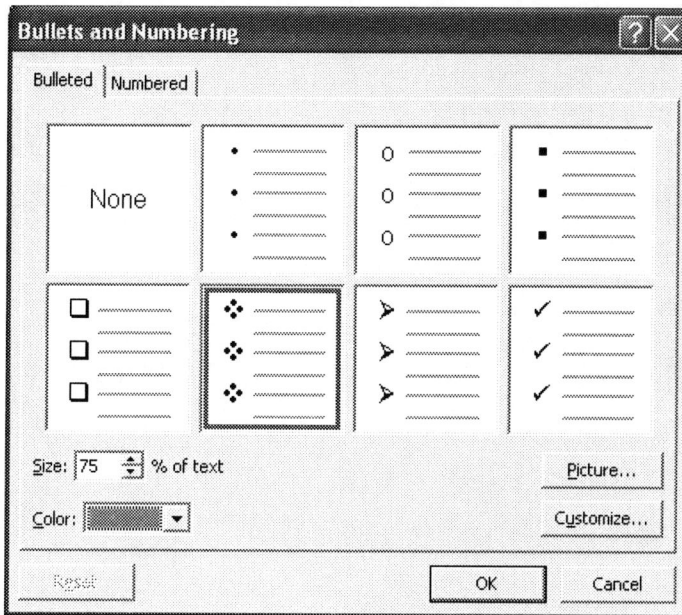

■ Click **OK**.

Inserting another character as a bullet

■ Go to the **Bullets and Numbering** dialog box with **Format - Bullets and Numbering - Bulleted** tab.

■ Click the **Customize** button.

■ In the **Font** list, choose the required character font.

■ Click the character/symbol of your choice.

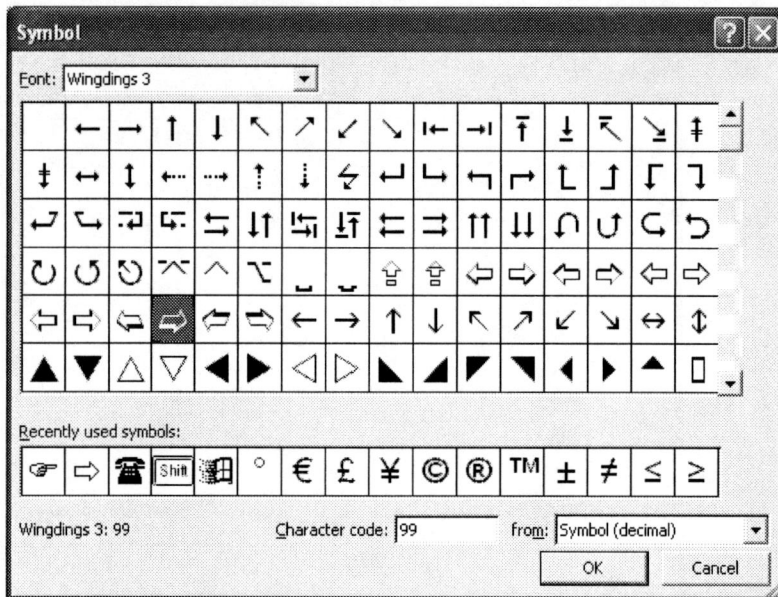

The symbol's decimal code appears in the **Character code** box.

* Confirm with **OK**.

  You return to the **Bullets and Numbering** dialog box. The last bullet style shown is now called **Custom**.

* If required, choose the bullet's **Size** and/or **Color**.

* Click **OK** to confirm.

Inserting a picture as a bullet

* **Format - Bullets and Numbering - Bulleted** tab

* Click the **Picture** button.

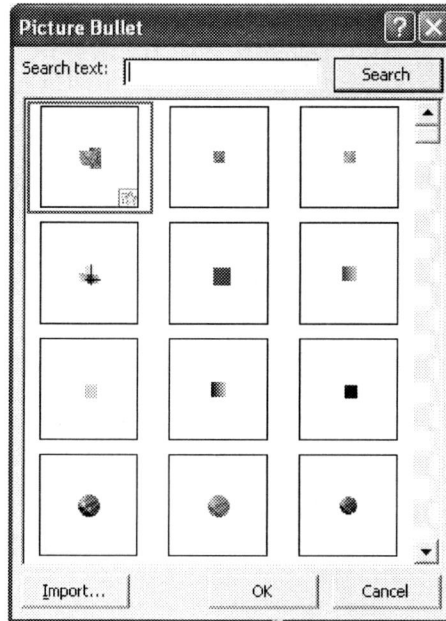

» Select a picture then click **OK** to insert the bullet.

⊞8 ▪ Modifying paragraph alignment

» Select all the paragraphs that should have the same alignment or click the paragraph you wish to align. If you want to make changes to all the paragraphs of a particular level, go to the slide master and click the level concerned.

» Use one of these techniques:

Alignment	🖱	📦
Left alignment	≣	Ctrl **L**
Centre alignment	≣	Ctrl **E**
Right alignment	≣	Ctrl **R**
Justified text	≣	Ctrl **J**

> You will also find these alignment options in *Format - Alignment*.

▣ 9 ▪ Modifying spacing between and within paragraphs

▪ Select the paragraphs concerned. If you want to make changes to all the paragraphs of a particular level, go to the slide master and click the level concerned.

▪ **Format - Line Spacing**

▪ In the **Line spacing** frame, select the unit of measurement (**Lines** or **Points**) then indicate how much space to leave between the lines you have selected.

▪ Using the **Before paragraph** and/or **After paragraph** options, indicate how much space to leave around the paragraphs and choose the unit of measurement required (again you can use lines or points).

▪ Confirm by clicking **OK**.

Below you can see **Practice Exercise** 2.2. This exercise is made up of 9 steps. If you do not know how to do one of the steps, go back to the title that corresponds to that particular lesson. When you have finished, you can check your work by reading the **Solution** that follows.

All the steps in this exercise are likely to be tested in the MOUS exam.

☞ Practice Exercise 2.2

*To work on exercise 2.2, you should open the **2-2 Skating.ppt** presentation in the **MOUS PowerPoint 2002** folder.*

1. On the first slide, apply to the text **Rollerbladers** the **Comic Sans MS** font; if this font is not available on your computer, use another of your choice.

2. Replace the **Arial** font by **Tahoma**.

3. Make the **Rollerbladers** text appear with a **48** font size.

4. Apply a **Bold** text attribute to the characters in the text **A great sport for all** on the opening slide.

5. Apply the **Shadow Style 14** to the text in the subtitle placeholder on the first slide (**Inline Skating Club - A great sport for all**).

6. Apply a light green colour to the characters **Roller** in the text **Roller-bladers** on the first slide and to the text **Inline Skating Club** in the subtitle of the same slide.

7. Activate the last slide in the presentation and apply bullets to all the paragraphs in the slide body text, using the ❖ character as the bullet.

8. Centre the title of the last slide in the presentation.

9. Select a spacing of 0.5 lines, to be used before all the paragraphs in the body text of the last slide.
Finish by saving and closing the presentation.

If you want to put what you have learnt into practice on a real document, you can work on summary exercise 2 for the WORKING WITH TEXT section, that you can find at the end of this book.

It is often possible to perform a task in several different ways, but here only the easiest solution is presented. You can go back to the corresponding lesson if you want to see other techniques you could use.

Solution to Exercise 2.2

1. To apply the Comic Sans MS font to the text "Rollerbladers", select the text **Rollerbladers** by dragging over it.
   Open the **Font** list on the **Formatting** toolbar and, if necessary, scroll down the list until you see the **Comic Sans MS** font. Click the font to select it.

2. To replace the Arial font by Tahoma, click outside all placeholders. Use the **Format - Replace Fonts** command. Open the **Replace** list and ensure that **Arial** is selected. In the **With** list, choose **Tahoma**.
   Click the **Replace** button then the **Close** button.

3. To give the text "Rollerbladers" a font size of 48, drag to select the characters, open the **Font Size** list on the **Formatting** toolbar then click **48**.

4. To apply bold type to the characters in the text "A great sport for all" on the opening slide, drag to select these characters then click the **B** tool button on the **Formatting** toolbar.

5. To apply the shadow style 14 to the text in the subtitle placeholder on the first slide, click this placeholder. Click the tool button on the **Drawing** toolbar then click the **Shadow Style 14** (point to each style until its name appears in a ScreenTip). To see the effect produced, click outside the placeholder.

6. To apply a light green colour to the characters "Roller" in the word Rollerbladers on the first slide, drag to select that part of the word. Open the list on the **A** tool button on the **Drawing** or **Formatting** toolbar and choose the light green colour (the sixth colour in the top row). Next, to apply the same colour to the text "Inline Skating Club" in the subtitle, select the text **Inline Skating Club** and click the **A** tool button to apply the light green colour.

7. To activate the last slide in the 2-2 Skating presentation, click its icon on the **Slides** tab. To apply bullets to all the paragraphs in the slide body text, using the ❖ character as the bullet, select all the paragraphs in the body of the slide (starting from **Aggressive**). Use the **Format - Bullets and Numbering** command. On the **Bulleted** tab, click the ❖ type of bullet (second row, second bullet) then click **OK**.

8. To centre the title of the last slide in the presentation, click the **Club activities** paragraph then click the ▤ tool button on the **Formatting** toolbar to align the text in the centre of the paragraph.

9. To apply a 0.5 line spacing before all the paragraphs in the body text of slide 3, select the text from **Aggressive** to **Family rollerblading**.
Activate the **Format - Line Spacing** command then, if necessary, choose the unit **Lines** in the **Before paragraph** list and enter **0.5** in the accompanying text box. Enter.
To save and close the presentation, use **File - Close** and click **Yes** when PowerPoint asks you if you want to save the presentation.

USING TEMPLATES
Lesson 3.1: Design templates

1 ▪ Applying a design template

A design template contains formatting elements such as font, font size, backgrounds and colour schemes. When you apply a design template, you automatically apply a slide master. You can use several templates in the same presentation.

▪ Select the group of slides to which you want to apply the template or, if you are applying the template to the whole presentation, do not select anything.

▪ Open the **Slide Design** task pane or use **Format - Slide Design** or ![Design].

*Templates are classified in three categories: **Used in This Presentation, Recently Used** and **Available For Use.***

▪ To enlarge the design template previews, point to one of the templates, open its list and choose the **Show Large Previews** option.

On the template's drop-down menu, you can see the **Apply to Selected Slides** and **Apply to All Slides** options, which let you choose to which part of the presentation the template will be applied. You must use this menu to apply a template to a single slide, for example. When several templates are used in the one presentation, another option appears, called **Apply to Master**. This option applies a template to a group of slides that currently use a different template, but you need select only one slide in that group.

* Click the template to apply it to the selected slides or to the whole presentation (if you made no prior selection) and to the slide master.

The template now appears in the **Used in This Presentation** list. The **Default Design** that creates a blank presentation appears first in the **Available For Use** list.

> If you want to modify a design template, you need to modify its elements (the slide master, the background and so on).
>
> If the template you want to use does not appear in the **Slide Design** task pane, click the **Browse** link to access the **Templates** folder in **C:\Windows\Application Data\Microsoft** or in **C:\Documents and Settings\Username\Application Data\Microsoft**, according to your operating system. If necessary, open the subfolder containing the template you want to use and double-click its name.

> To apply a template to a single slide, you must select the slide in the **Slides** tab, point to the template you wish to use then open the drop-down menu with the arrow that appears and choose the **Apply to Selected Slides** option.

2 • Creating a design template

* Open or create the presentation on which you want to base your template.
* Using the various masters, create all the items that you want to include in your template.

* **File - Save As**

* If necessary, give a name for the template.

* Open the **Save as type** list and choose the **Design Template** option.

  *This option automatically opens the **Templates** folder in **C:\Windows\Application Data\Microsoft** or in **C:\Documents and Settings\Username\Application Data\ Microsoft**, according to your operating system. This is where templates are saved by default.*

* Click the **Save** button.

  📄 *Design templates always have a .pot file extension (however, file extensions may not always be visible on your computer).*

  *If you use Microsoft Office, the various design templates supplied with PowerPoint 2002 are stored in **C:\Program Files\Microsoft Office\ Templates\Presentation Designs**.*

  *Any templates you create will be visible in the **Slide Design** task pane the next time you open PowerPoint, classified in the **Available For Use** category.*

Below you can see **Practice Exercise** 3.1. This exercise is made up of 2 steps. If you do not know how to do one of the steps, go back to the title that corresponds to that particular lesson. When you have finished, you can check your work by reading the **Solution** that follows.

All the steps in this exercise are likely to be tested in the MOUS exam.

☞ Practice Exercise 3.1

*To work on exercise 3.1, you should open the **3-1 Triathlon.ppt** presentation in the **MOUS PowerPoint 2002** folder.*

1. To all the slides in the presentation, apply the design template called **Blends**. Next, apply the template called **Ocean** to slides **3** and **4**. Next, apply the template **Glass Layers** to slide **5** and the template **Edge** to slide **6**.

2. Delete slide **4** and all the text in the presentation then from that result, save the presentation as a design template called **3-1 Triathlon.pot**, into the **Templates** folder. Finish by closing the **3-1 Triathlon.pot** file.

If you want to put what you have learnt into practice on a real document, you can work on summary exercise 3 for the USING TEMPLATES section, that you can find at the end of this book.

USING TEMPLATES
Exercise 3.1: Design templates

It is often possible to perform a task in several different ways, but here only the easiest solution is presented. You can go back to the corresponding lesson if you want to see other techniques you could use.

Solution to Exercise 3.1

1. To apply the design template called "Blends" to all the slides in the presentation, start by clicking the [Design] tool button to open the **Slide Design** task pane.
   Do not select any slides, and in the **Available For Use** category on the **Slide Design** task pane, click the **Blends** design template (note that the templates are arranged in alphabetical order and each template's name appears in a ScreenTip if you point to it).
   To apply the template called "Ocean" to slides 3 and 4, [Shift]-click slides **3** and **4** in the **Slides** tab to select them then in the **Available For Use** category, click the **Ocean** template.
   To apply the template "Glass Layers" to slide 5, click slide **5** in the **Slides** tab to select it then in the **Available For Use** category, point to the **Glass Layers** template, click the arrow that appears to open its drop-down menu and choose the **Apply to Selected Slides** option.
   To apply the template "Edge" to slide 6, click slide **6** in the **Slides** tab to select it then in the **Available For Use** category, point to the **Edge** template, click the arrow that appears to open its drop-down menu and choose the **Apply to Selected Slides** option.

2. To delete slide 4 from the presentation, click it in the **Slides** tab and press the [Del] key.
   To delete all the text in the presentation, carry out the following actions for each slide:
   - select the slide by clicking it in the **Slides** tab,
   - in the slide pane, click the slide, taking care not to click in any place-holder,

- use the **Edit - Select All** command and press the ⌜Del⌟ key.

To save the result of this as a design template called 3-1 Triathlon.pot, use the **File - Save As** command. Open the **Save as type** list and choose the **Design Template** option in this list. Keep the proposed **File name** and click the **Save** button.

To finish, close the **3-1 Triathlon.pot** template with **File - Close**.

USING TEMPLATES
Lesson 3.2: Template elements

▥1 ▪ Modifying the different masters

PowerPoint presentations include design template information (such as font styles, placeholder sizes and positions, backgrounds and colour schemes). PowerPoint stores such information in an element called a **master**. Each presentation has at least three masters: the slide master, the handout master and the notes master.

Modifying the slide master

The slide master allows you to alter all the slides in the presentation (by adding objects and changing fonts or footers, for example). The template generally contains a title master also. When you modify the title master, you affect the slides that have a **Title Slide** layout.

» **View - Master - Slide Master** or hold down the ⸢Shift⸥ key and click ▣ at the base of the tabs pane.

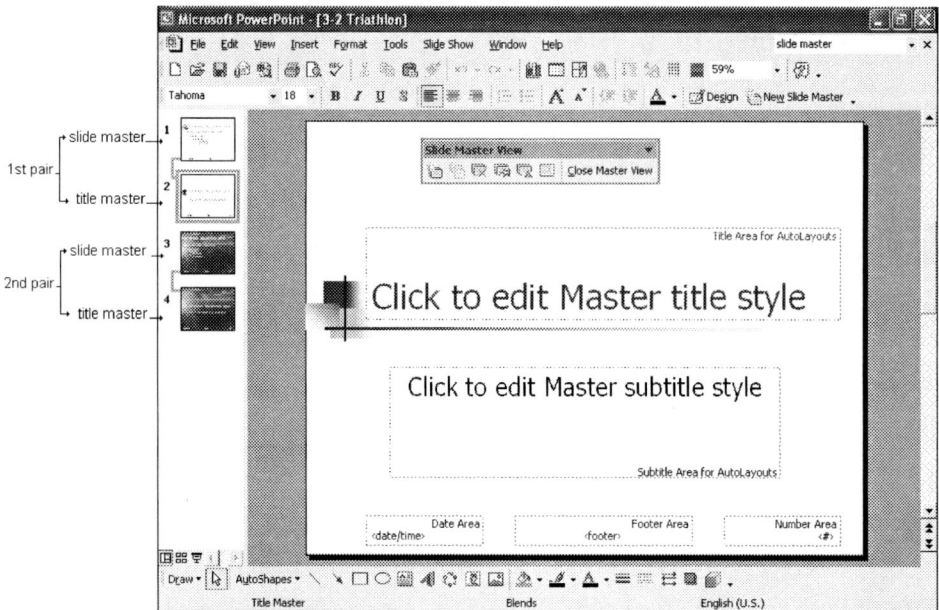

The **Slide Master View** *toolbar appears. If several different design templates have been applied to the presentation, there will be several slide and title masters (one pair for each design template applied). Consequently, if you wish to make a modification that will apply to the whole presentation, you must modify each pair of slide and/or title masters.*

* In the left-hand pane, select the thumbnail of the master you want to change.

  When you point to a master thumbnail, PowerPoint indicates its name and the slides to which it applies. The status bar indicates the active master.

* Make your required changes (such as changing the fonts or font styles, editing or deleting placeholders, changing the background, changing the colour scheme and so on).

Modifying the handout master

The handout master allows you to alter the sizes, positions and formatting of header and footer placeholders. Changes you make to this master appear when you print your handout or outline.

* **View - Master - Handout Master** or hold down the ⌗Shift⌗ key and click 🏛 at the base of the tabs pane.

USING TEMPLATES

Lesson 3.2: Template elements

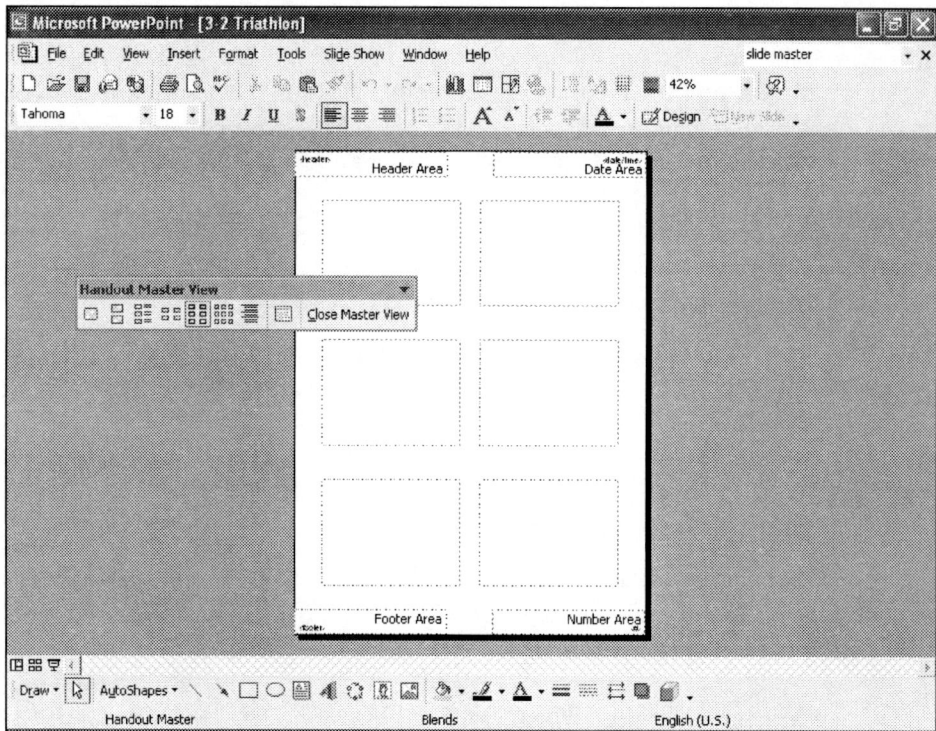

*The status bar confirms that you are in the **Handout Master** and the **Handout Master View** toolbar appears.*

* Using the tool buttons on the **Handout Master View** toolbar, indicate the required layout for all the pages in the handout.

* Carry out your modifications (create a header or footer, insert objects, and so on).

* To apply a background fill, use the **Format - Handout Background** command.

When you customise handouts, the changes also apply to printed outlines.

*To preview a customised handout, go into the print preview and in the **Print What** list, choose one of the **Handouts** options. To print the customised handout, choose the **Handouts** option in the **Print what** list in the **Print** dialog box.*

118

Modifying the notes master

The notes master allows you to resize and position slide and notes placeholders, to add drawing objects and to modify the colours of backgrounds and notes pages.

* **View - Master - Notes Master**

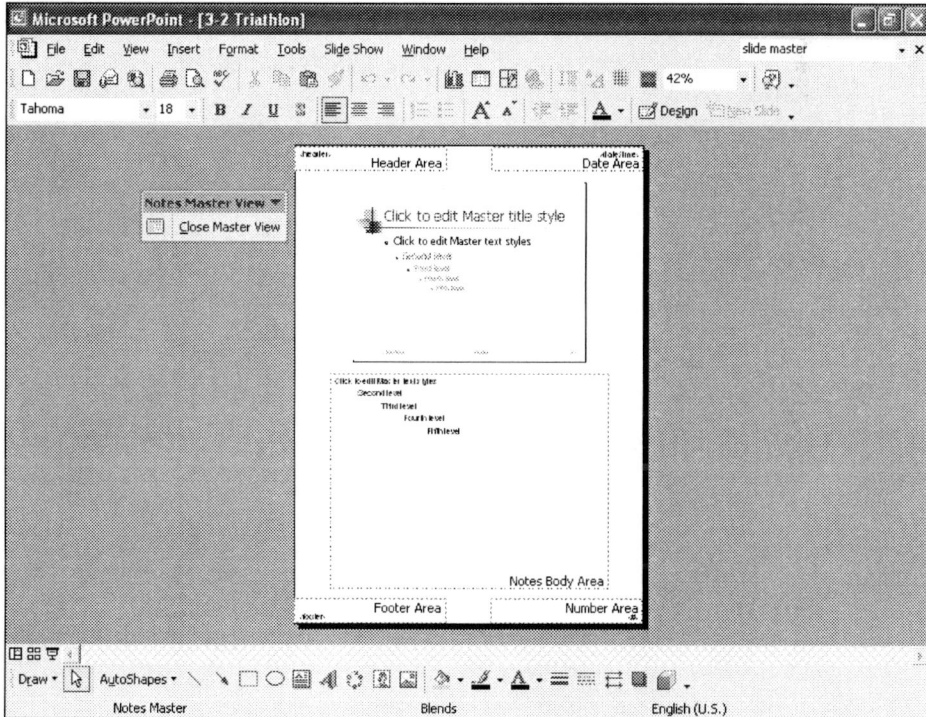

*The status bar confirms that you are in the **Notes Master** and the **Notes Master View** toolbar appears.*

* Make your required changes (creating a header, footer, inserting objects and so on).

* To apply a background fill, use the **Format - Notes Background** command.

Changes you make to this master appear in the notes pages display and print preview.

📄 *To preview and/or print customised notes, choose the **Notes Pages** option in the **Print What** list in the print preview or the **Print what** list in the **Print** dialog box.*

Closing the master view

※ To close a master view, click the **Close Master View** tool button or select another view.

🖥 2 ▪ Managing placeholders

Placeholders appear in master views as areas bordered by dotted lines (title areas, subtitle areas, text areas, notes areas, date areas, number areas and footer areas).

※ Activate the master of your choice.

Modifying a placeholder

※ To select a placeholder, point to it so that the mouse pointer appears as a four-headed arrow then click.

※ You can modify colours, lines and sizes, etc., as you would for any other object. You can also use the **Format - Placeholder** command and use the different pages of the dialog box.

Deleting a placeholder

※ Select the placeholder you want to delete.

※ **Edit - Clear** or Del

Restoring a deleted placeholder

» **Format - Master Layout** or 🔲

» Activate the check box corresponding to the deleted placeholder you wish to restore.

» Click **OK**.

🏠3 ▪ **Applying a colour scheme to slides**

A colour scheme is made up of eight colours. These are the colours for the background, text and lines, shadows, title text, fills, accents and hyperlinks.

» By default, your colour scheme will apply to all the slides that are based on the design template of the active slide. To apply your colour scheme to only a few slides, select the slides concerned in Normal view. If your presentation uses more than one design template, select the group of slides concerned or one slide in the group that uses a particular template, if you wish to change that entire group of slides.

» Display the **Slide Design** task pane using **Format - Slide Design** or 🖉 Design .

» At the top of the task pane, click the **Color Schemes** link.

The colour schemes that appear under ***Apply a color scheme*** *depend on the design template applied to the slides selected in the* ***Slides*** *tab.*

▪ Click the required colour scheme to apply it to either the slides you selected at the start or to all the slides of a particular template,
or
point to the required colour scheme, click the arrow to open its list and choose:

Apply to Master — to apply the colour scheme to all the slides based on a given design template.

Apply to All Slides — to apply the colour scheme to all the slides in the presentation, no matter what templates are used.

Apply to Selected Slides — to apply the colour scheme to a selection of slides or to a single slide.

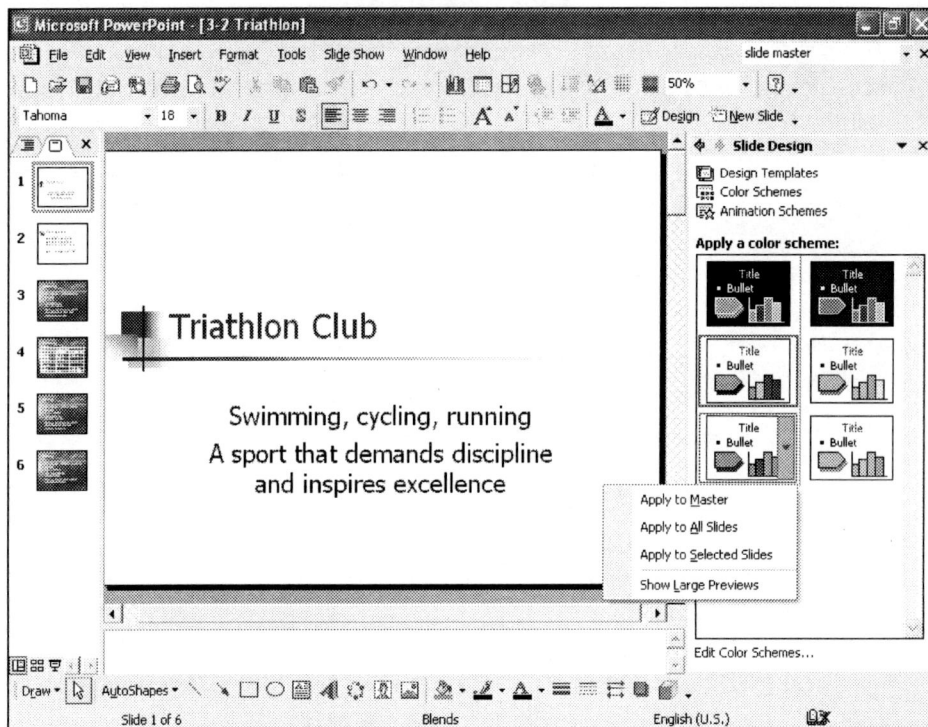

📄 *You can apply a notes page and/or handout colour scheme in the same way. To apply a notes page colour scheme, go into Notes Page view or Notes Master view (if you want to apply your colour scheme to all the pages) and apply the required colour scheme. To apply a handout colour scheme, go into Handout Master view and apply the required colour scheme.*

4 • Managing colour schemes

Modifying a colour scheme

» In the **Slide Design** task pane, click the **Edit Color Schemes** link.

» Under the **Custom** tab, choose the colour you want to modify in the **Scheme colors** frame.

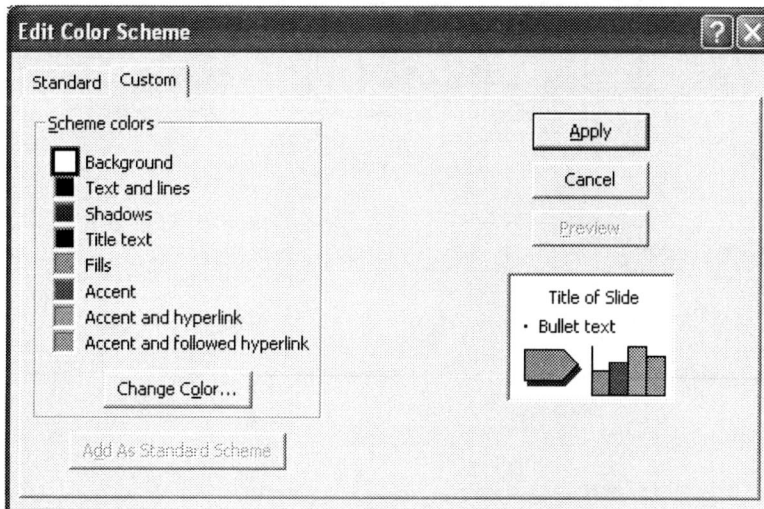

» Click the **Change Color** button.

» Carry out one of the following actions:

- Under the **Standard** tab, select the required colour.

- Under the **Custom** tab, drag the pointer in the form of a cross to select a colour then drag the vertical slider to adjust the luminosity of your selected colour.

» Click **OK**.

*The colour you selected in the **Scheme colors** frame is modified accordingly. Click the **Preview** button to view the effect of your changes without leaving the **Edit Color Scheme** dialog box.*

» Modify any of the other colours in the **Scheme colors** frame in the same way.

» Click the **Apply** button.

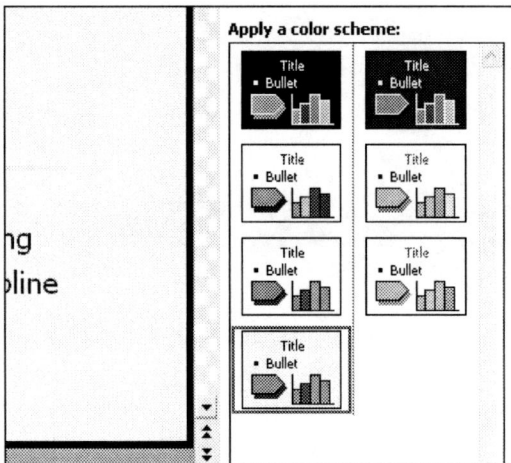

When you modify a colour scheme, PowerPoint creates a new colour scheme and includes it in the **Color Schemes** library of the **Slide Design** task pane.

📄 *You can use up to 16 colour schemes for each design template in a presentation.*

Deleting a colour scheme

» In the **Slide Design** task pane, click the **Edit Color Schemes** link.

» Select the **Standard** tab.

» In the **Color schemes** frame, click the scheme you want to delete.

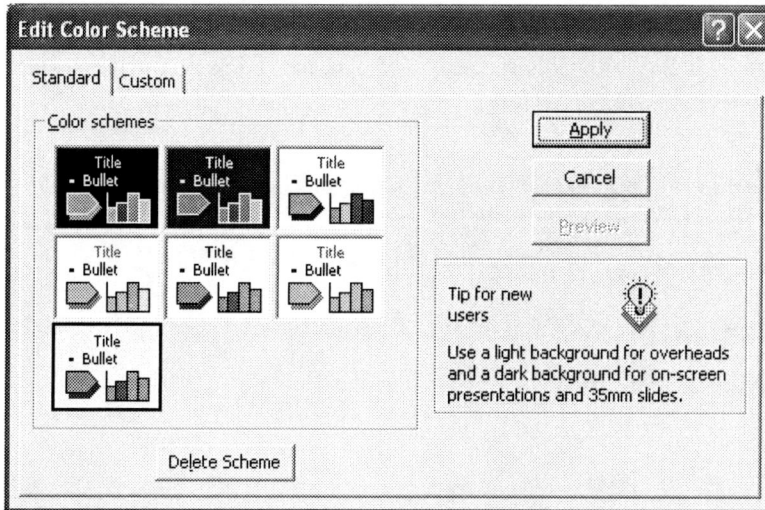

- Click the **Delete Scheme** button.

- In the **Color schemes** frame, select the colour scheme you want to apply then click the **Apply** button.

Using the colour scheme from another slide

You can use the colour scheme from another slide, either from the active presentation or from another presentation.

- Open the presentation(s) concerned.

- Display the **Slides** tab in Normal view in each presentation.

- Select the slide that contains the colour scheme you want to use.

- To copy the colour scheme to a single slide, click the tool button. To copy it to several slides, double-click the tool button.

- If you are copying to another presentation, open the **Window** menu and select the presentation you want to activate.

- To apply the copied colour scheme to a single slide, click the slide concerned. To apply the colour scheme to several slides, click each of the slides concerned and press Esc when you have finished.

> When you copy a slide's colour scheme to another presentation, PowerPoint includes the colour scheme in the **Slide Design - Color Schemes** task pane of the other presentation.

5 • Changing the slide background colour

- If you do not want to apply your modifications to all the slides, select the slides concerned in Normal view.

- **Format - Background**

- Open the **Background fill** list.

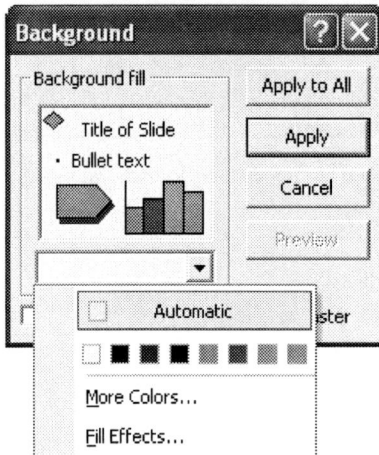

The **Automatic** option will re-apply the background fill from the template. The **Preview** button lets you see the effect produced without closing the dialog box.

- Click one of the colours displayed in this list. If you do not want to use any of these colours, select the **More Colors** option.

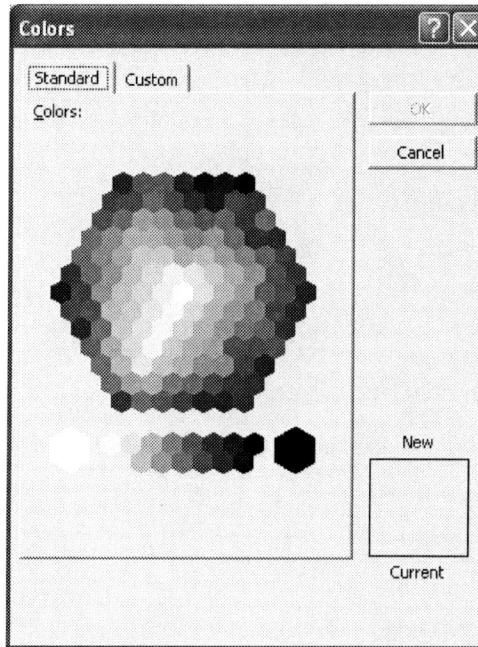

▪ Choose a colour under the **Standard** tab or create your own colour under the **Custom** tab.

▪ Click **OK**.

▪ Click the **Apply** button to change only the selected slide(s) or click the **Apply to All** button to apply the changes to all the slides and to the corresponding master.

📄 *You can change the background colour of handouts and/or notes pages in the same way. For notes pages, go into Notes Page view or into the Notes Master and use the* **Format - Notes Background** *command. To modify handouts, go into the Handout Master and use* **Format - Handout Background***.*

▣6 ▪ Changing a slide's background fill

- If you want to modify only certain slides, select them in Normal view.
- **Format - Background**
- Open the drop-down list in the **Background fill** frame and click the **Fill Effects** option.

Applying a gradient as a background fill

- If necessary, activate the **Gradient** tab in the **Fill Effects** dialog box.
- In the **Colors** frame, choose:

One color	to fill the slides with a single colour; choose the colour in the **Color 1** list and set its intensity with the **Dark/Light** slider.
Two colors	to fill the slide with a gradient that starts at one colour and finishes at another; choose the required colours in the **Color 1** and **Color 2** lists,
Preset	to fill the slide with a predefined gradient; choose the required effect in the **Preset colors** list (this list is not in alphabetical order).

- In the **Shading styles** frame, choose the look of the gradient, using the **Variants** shown to guide you.
- Click the variant you want to apply.

» Click **OK**.

» Choose to **Apply** the gradient to the selected slides or to **Apply to All** including the master.

Applying a texture as a background fill

» If necessary, activate the **Texture** tab in the **Fill Effects** dialog box.

» Select the texture you wish to apply.

*The name of the texture appears under the texture swatches and a **Sample** of the effect is shown.*

- Confirm with **OK**.

- Choose to **Apply** the texture to the selected slides or to **Apply to All** including the master.

Applying a pattern as a background fill

- If necessary, activate the **Pattern** tab in the **Fill Effects** dialog box.

- Select the pattern you wish to apply.

  *Once you click a pattern, its name appears and a **Sample** of the effect is shown.*

- If necessary, choose the **Foreground** and **Background** colours.

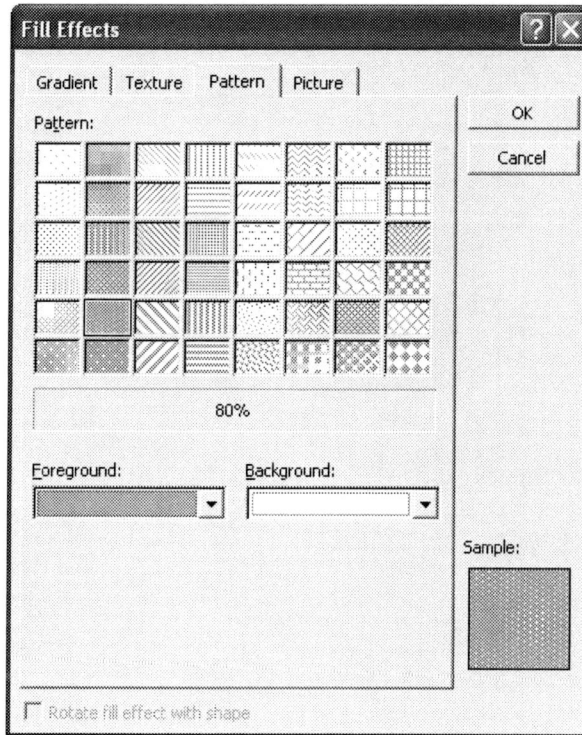

- Click **OK**.
- Choose to **Apply** the pattern to the selected slides or to **Apply to All** including the master.

Inserting a picture as a background fill

- If necessary, activate the **Picture** tab in the **Fill Effects** dialog box.
- Click the **Select Picture** button.
- Choose where the picture file is stored and double-click the name of the picture you want to use.

*The picture appears, along with its name and a **Sample** of how it will look on the slide.*

⊗ Click **OK** and choose to **Apply** the picture to the selected slides or to **Apply to All** including the master.

▣7 ▪ Hiding background graphics

You may find it useful to hide the slide background graphics linked to the template or the master.

⊗ If you want to work on only a few slides, select them.

⊗ **Format - Background**

⊗ Tick the **Omit background graphics from master** check box.

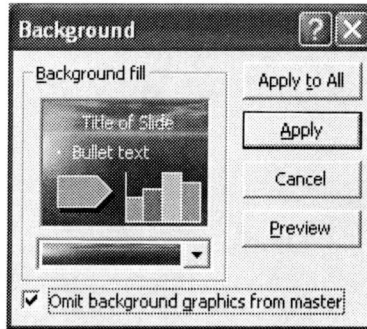

- Click **Apply** to modify only the slide you selected or **Apply to All** to change all the slides in the presentation.

8 ▪ Working with slide masters

- Go into Slide Master view using **View - Master - Slide Master** or hold down the [Shift] key while you click the ⊞ symbol at the base of the tabs pane.

Adding a slide master

- Click the 🖻 tool button on the **Slide Master View** toolbar to add a slide master that uses the default styles,
  or
  click below the other master(s) in the **Slides** tab to position the insertion point and click the [🖉 Design] button on the **Formatting** toolbar. Click the required design template to add a slide master with that design,
  or
  click below the other master(s) in the **Slides** tab, choose a design template and open its drop-down menu and choose the **Add Design** option.

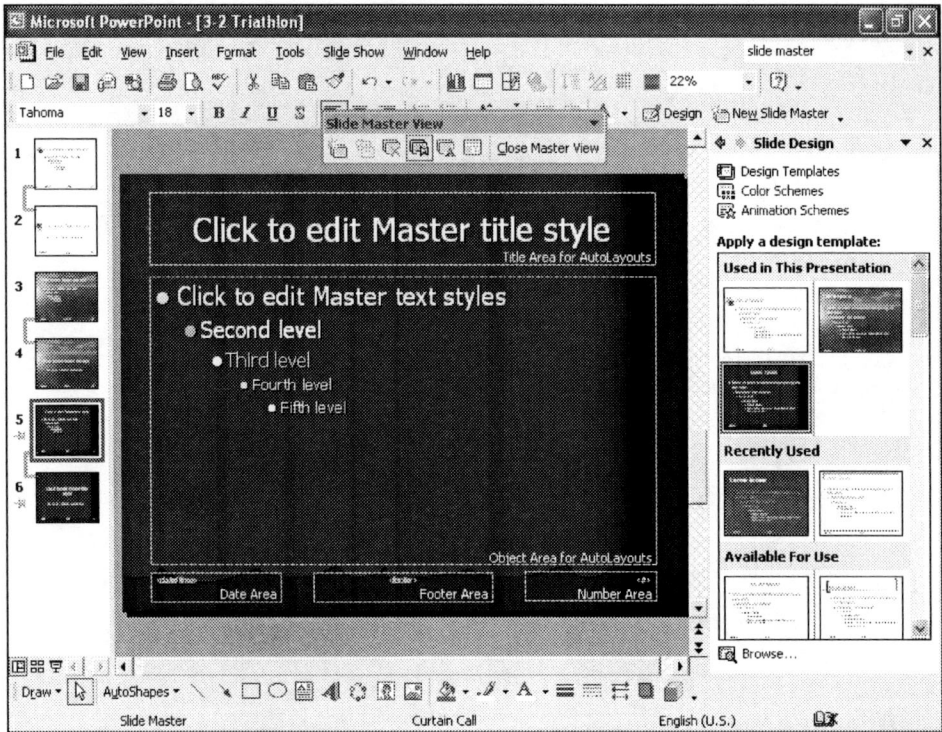

The new master appears in the left pane. Masters created in this way are protected from automatic deletion (the "protected" symbol appears to their left).

A design template (called **Custom Design** on masters using the default styles) appears in the **Slide Design - Design Templates** task pane, in the **Used in This Presentation** category. This design template can then be applied to any slide you wish (in Normal view).

To insert a title master for an existing slide master, select the slide master thumbnail on the left and click the ⌷ tool button on the **Slide Master View** toolbar.

Deleting a slide master or a title master

When you delete a slide master, the accompanying title master is deleted automatically.

※ Select the master you want to delete by clicking its thumbnail in the left pane.

※ Click the [icon] tool button on the **Slide Master View** toolbar.

Preventing the deletion of slide masters

When you delete all the slides based on a master or when you apply a different design template to all those slides, PowerPoint automatically deletes the slide master concerned. However, you can "protect" a master, to prevent it from being deleted automatically.

※ Select the master you want to protect by clicking its thumbnail in the left pane.

※ Click the [icon] tool button on the **Slide Master View** toolbar.

※ To remove the protection, simply click the same tool button again.

> [icon] *You can manually delete a master, even if it is protected.*
>
> *On a pair of slide and title masters, protecting one automatically protects the other.*

Renaming a slide master

※ Select the master you want to rename by clicking its thumbnail in the left pane.

※ Click the [icon] tool button on the **Slide Master View** toolbar.

Rename Master

Master name:
Blends

Rename

Cancel

» In the **Master name** box, enter the new name and click the **Rename** button.

📄 *On a pair of slide and title masters, renaming one automatically renames the other.*

Below you can see **Practice Exercise** 3.2. This exercise is made up of 8 steps. If you do not know how to do one of the steps, go back to the title that corresponds to that particular lesson. When you have finished, you can check your work by reading the **Solution** that follows.

Steps that are likely to be tested during the MOUS exam are marked with this symbol: ⊞. However, it is a good idea to complete the whole exercise to ensure you have understood everything covered in the lesson.

☞ Practice Exercise 3.2

To work on exercise 3.2, you should open the presentation called **3-2 Triathlon.ppt** *in the* **MOUS PowerPoint 2002** *folder.*

⊞ 1. Activate the Slide Master view and select the **Ocean** slide master to give a ✓ bullet, in navy blue, to all the first level paragraphs. Next, leave the slide master to see the effect produced on slides 3, 5 and 6 in the presentation.

⊞ 2. Go into Slide Master view and select the slide master called **Ocean**. On this master, select the **Footer Area** placeholder and give it a yellow text colour. Leave slide master view.

⊞ 3. On the first two slides in the presentation, apply the colour scheme in the third row of the first column of schemes offered in the task pane.

4. Modify the background colour of the colour scheme chosen in step 3. Instead of white, choose a pale yellow colour.

⊞ 5. Modify the background colour of the first two slides. Choose the colour purple.

⊞ 6. Choose the texture called **Parchment** for the background of the first two slides.

⊞ 7. Hide the background graphics on the last four slides.

8. Add a slide master using the design template called **Curtain Call**. Rename the slide master used on the first two slides (change it from **Blends** to **Triathlon Blends**). Leave Slide Master view and apply the master added with the **Curtain Call** design to the last two slides in the presentation. Save and close the presentation.

If you want to put what you have learnt into practice on a real document, you can work on summary exercise 3 for the USING TEMPLATES section, that you can find at the end of this book.

It is often possible to perform a task in several different ways, but here only the easiest solution is presented. You can go back to the corresponding lesson if you want to see other techniques you could use.

Solution to Exercise 3.2

1. To activate the Slide Master view and select the Ocean slide master, hold down the [Shift] key and click the 🖽 tool button. Click the thumbnail called **Ocean Slide Master** (if you point to each master, its name appears in a ScreenTip).

   To give a ✓ bullet, in navy blue, to all the first level paragraphs, click **Click to edit Master text styles** in the placeholder and use the **Format - Bullets and Numbering** command. In the **Bulleted** tab, choose the ✓ bullet type then open the **Color** list and choose the navy blue colour (the first colour swatch). Click **OK**.

   To leave Slide Master view, click the **Close Master View** button on the **Slide Master View** toolbar then click slide **3**, **5** and **6** to see the effects.

2. To activate the Slide Master view and select the Ocean slide master, hold down the [Shift] key and click the 🖽 tool button. If necessary, click the thumbnail called **Ocean Slide Master**.

   To select the **Footer Area** placeholder, click it in the master.

   To give that placeholder a yellow text colour, open the list on the 🅐▾ button and click the yellow colour (the second to last colour).
   To leave the Slide Master view, click the **Close Master View** button on the **Slide Master View** toolbar.

3. To apply the colour scheme in the third row of the first column of schemes offered in the task pane to the first two slides, click the thumbnail of the first slide or select the first two slides. Click the [Design] button then click the **Color Schemes** link on the task pane. Click the colour scheme in the list (first column, third row; make sure you are not displaying large previews).

4. To modify the background colour of the colour scheme chosen in step 3, click the **Edit Color Schemes** link at the bottom of the **Slide Design - Color Schemes** task pane. On the **Custom** page, make sure **Background** is selected in the **Scheme colors** frame then click the **Change Color** button. On the **Standard** page, click the pale yellow swatch on the colour picker (this is just below the white swatch in the centre).
Click **OK** then click **Apply**.

5. To modify the background colour of the first two slides, start by selecting them. Activate the **Format - Background** command then open the list box in the **Background fill** frame and choose purple (the second to last colour).
Click the **Apply** button.

6. To choose the "Parchment" texture as the background fill for the first two slides, start by selecting the slides, if necessary. Activate the **Format - Background** command then open the list box in the **Background fill** frame. Choose the **Fill Effects** option and click the **Texture** tab. Click the texture called **Parchment** (point to see each texture's name in a ScreenTip). Click **OK** then the **Apply** button.

7. To hide the background graphics on the last four slides, select those slides. Use the **Format - Background** command and tick the **Omit background graphics from master** check box. Click **Apply**.

8. To add a slide master using the design template called Curtain Call, hold down the [Shift] key and click [⊞] to open Slide Master view. Click below the other masters in the **Slides** tab to position the insertion point. Point to the **Curtain Call** design template in the task pane: an arrow appears on its right. Click this arrow and in the drop-down menu, click the **Add Design** option.

To rename the slide master used on the first two slides, select the master called **Blends** by clicking its thumbnail in the left pane then click the [⌷] tool button on the **Slide Master View** toolbar.
Enter **Triathlon Blends** and click the **Rename** button.

To leave Slide Master view, click the **Close Master View** button on the **Slide Master View** toolbar.

To apply the master added with the Curtain Call design on the last two slides in the presentation, select these last two slides then click the **Curtain Call** design template in the **Used in This Presentation** category on the **Slide Design - Design Templates** task pane.

To save and close the presentation, use **File - Close** and click **Yes** when PowerPoint asks you if you want to save the presentation.

CREATING AND MODIFYING OBJECTS
Lesson 4.1: Drawing objects

CREATING AND MODIFYING OBJECTS
Lesson 4.1: Drawing objects

🖾 1 ▪ Drawing an oval/a rectangle/a straight line or an arrow

- Activate the slide in which you want to make the drawing.

- If it is hidden, show the **Drawing** toolbar and use these tools:

  - ↘ to draw a **Line**.

  - ↘ to draw an **Arrow**.

  - ☐ to draw a **Rectangle** (or square).

  - ○ to draw an **Oval** (or circle).

- Position the pointer (which becomes a black cross) at the place where you wish to start (or finish) the drawing.

- Draw the shape using one of the following techniques:

  - Click the workspace to draw a shape of predefined size.

  - Drag to draw the shape.

  - Hold down the [Shift] key and drag to draw a horizontal, vertical or oblique line or arrow, or a perfectly proportioned square or circle.

  - Hold down the [Ctrl] key and drag to draw the shape from its central point.

WESTPORT ARTS AND CRAFTS CENTRE

Once you have drawn a shape, it is selected automatically. The white handles around the shape are resizing handles and the green handle is the rotation handle.

- If you have drawn an ellipse or a rectangle, enter a text if you wish and press [Esc].

Once you have finished a drawing, you return to object selection mode. If you want to draw several of the same object, double-click the drawing tool as you select it; make as many drawings as required then press Esc *to deactivate the tool and return to object selection mode.*

The colours applied depend on the current colour scheme, which is very often linked to the template being used.

If you have drawn one object on top of another, you can change the object stacking order, using the **Order** *options in the* **Draw** *list on the* **Drawing** *toolbar.*

2 ▪ Drawing an AutoShape

PowerPoint 2002 offers you a set of predefined drawing shapes, called AutoShapes (stars, speech bubbles, arrows etc.).

▪ Activate the slide in which you want to make the drawing.

▪ Open the **AutoShapes** list on the **Drawing** toolbar.

▪ Drag the pointer onto the category of your choice.

The AutoShapes are arranged into nine different categories. Each category offers a number of different shapes The **Lines, Connectors** *and* **Action Buttons** *categories contain shapes that are more unusual either because of what they do or how you draw them. The* **More AutoShapes** *category can be used to obtain other shapes in the form of picture clips.*

※ Point to the form you wish to draw (its name appears in a ScreenTip) and click to select the shape.

※ Draw the AutoShape either by dragging, with the [Shift] and/or [Ctrl] key(s) or with a single click to draw a predefined shape.

※ If you wish to put text in the shape, type it in.

※ Press [Esc] to confirm.

📄 *To replace one AutoShape with another, use the **Change AutoShape** option in the **Draw** list on the **Drawing** toolbar and choose the replacement shape.*

*When you select some AutoShapes, a yellow handle, called an **adjustment handle**, appears. To adjust the shape of the AutoShape, drag the adjustment handle in the required direction.*

3 ▪ Selecting objects

※ Go to the slide concerned.

※ To select a single object, point to it; when the mouse pointer appears as a four-headed arrow, click.

To select a placeholder, for example, you need to point to the edge to see the four-headed arrow.

※ To select several objects:

 - click to select the first object then [Shift]-click the other objects,
   or

 - if necessary, select the [▯] tool button and drag around all the objects you want to select.

※ To select all the objects on a slide:

 Edit - Select All or [Ctrl] **A**

4 ▪ Deleting objects

▪ Select the object or objects you want to delete.

▪ **Edit - Clear** or Del

5 ▪ Moving/copying objects

From one slide to another

▪ Select the object(s) you want to copy or move.

▪ To move the object(s):

Edit - Cut or ✂ or Ctrl **X**

To copy the object(s):

Edit - Copy or 📑 or Ctrl **C**

If you choose to move something, the selection of objects disappears. It is moved into the clipboard. If you are copying something, a copy of the selection is placed in the clipboard and the original selection remains in place.

▪ Go to the target slide where you wish to paste the selection.

▪ **Edit - Paste** or 📋 or Ctrl **V**

You can also use this technique to move objects from one presentation to another.

Within the same slide

▪ Select the object(s) you want to move or copy.

▪ Point to the selection and make sure that the pointer takes the form of a four-headed arrow.

▪ If you are moving a selection, drag it into its new position.

※ If you are copying a selection, hold down the ⌈Ctrl⌋ key and drag the selection to its new position (the pointer will be accompanied by a plus (+) sign). When you reach the required position, release the mouse button then the ⌈Ctrl⌋ key.

📄 *To position an object at a precise spot, open the **Format** menu and activate the option that corresponds to the object's name. Click the **Position** tab and give the object's **Horizontal** and/or **Vertical** position (from the area on the slide specified in the **From** box).*

*To copy one or more objects so that the copy is placed slightly to one side of the original, make your selection and choose **Edit - Duplicate**.*

🔍 *If you hold down the ⌈Shift⌋ key while you move a selection, the selection will move only in a perfectly vertical or horizontal line.*

6 ▪ Grouping/ungrouping objects

You can group related objects to make it easier to move them, format them and so on.

※ Select the objects you wish to group.

※ Open the **Draw** menu on the **Drawing** toolbar.

※ Click the **Group** option.

The objects are now grouped as a single object: selection handles appear at the edges of the group of objects.

※ To select one item within a group, click once to select the group then click a second time on the individual item you wish to select.

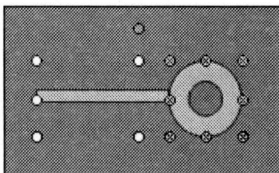

The selected item within the group appears with extra handles around it (these contain small crosses).

* To ungroup a group of objects, select the group then open the **Draw** list on the **Drawing** toolbar and click the **Ungroup** option.

> 📄 The **Regroup** option in the **Draw** list on the **Drawing** toolbar will regroup objects that you have ungrouped, without having to select them again.

7 ▪ Rotating an object or picture

Making a freehand rotation

* Select the object or picture you wish to rotate.

  A green handle appears above the selected object.

* Position the pointer on the green handle.

The pointer takes the shape of a circular arrow.

* Drag the pointer: the object will rotate in that direction.

> 📄 The same option can also be found via the **Format** menu: choose the option that corresponds to the object then click the **Size** tab and give a degree in the **Rotation** box.

Flipping an object or picture

* Select the object or picture you want to flip.

* Click the **Draw** button on the **Drawing** toolbar and choose the **Rotate or Flip** option.

* Choose the **Rotate Left** or **Rotate Right** option to turn the object on its side to the left or the right at a 90° angle,
  or
  choose the **Flip Horizontal** or **Flip Vertical** option to turn the selected object over at a 180° angle horizontally (from side to side) or vertically (from top to bottom).

📄 *The **Free Rotate** option can be used to rotate an object in any direction: activate it then drag any handle around the object's edge.*

You can also rotate a picture 90° to the left using the 🖼️ *tool button on the **Picture** toolbar.*

🪟8 ▪ Making freehand drawings

* Activate the slide concerned.

* Open the **AutoShapes** list on the **Drawing** toolbar and drag the pointer to the **Lines** category.

* Depending on your needs, click:

    🔲 to draw a series of curved segments (**Curve**).

    🔲 to draw a freeform, which can be a mixture of curved and straight segments (**Freeform**).

    🔲 to draw as if you were using a pencil (**Scribble**).

* Draw your drawing:

    - for a **Curve**, make a series of clicks with the mouse (the pointer takes the shape of a black cross).

    - for a **Freeform**, make successive clicks for the straight segments then drag when you want to create curves; when dragging, the mouse pointer takes the shape of a pen.

- for a **Scribble**, simply drag to draw (the pointer will again appear as a pen).

* To finish drawing a **Curve** or **Freeform**, double-click the place where you want to put the last point (for an open shape) or click back at the starting point (in which case the shape will be closed and coloured).

* To finish drawing a **Scribble**, release the mouse button.

The completed drawing is selected automatically and handles appear around it.

* To edit the points that determine the various segments of a drawing, select the drawing object and open the **Draw** list on the **Drawing** toolbar and choose the **Edit Points** option.

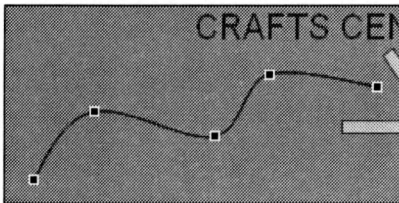

A point appears on each of the curves on the shape.

* If necessary, edit the shape:
drag a point to move it,
to delete a point, hold down `Ctrl` `Shift` and click the point,
to add a point, `Ctrl`-click the line.

* If you have finished working on the points, click outside the freehand drawing.

📕9 ▪ Inserting a WordArt object

WordArt applies special typographic effects to text. Here is an example:

* Activate the slide concerned.

* **Insert - Picture - WordArt** or

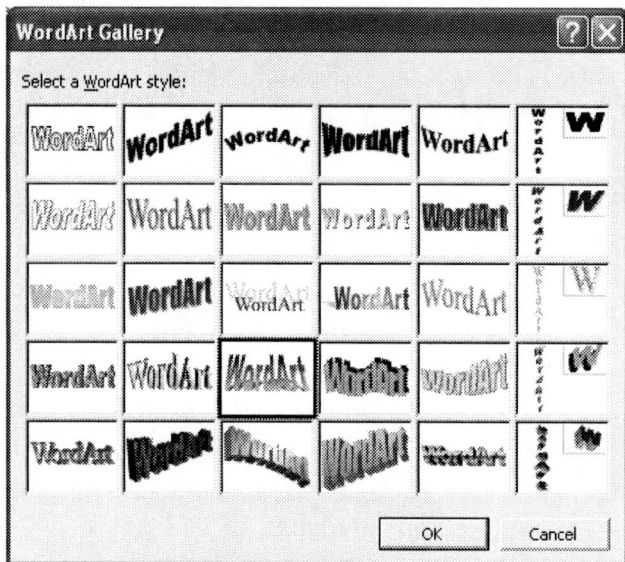

Each predefined effect contains its own formatting, font, font colour, character size, text orientation and so on. You can change these attributes at a later time.

» Double-click the effect you wish to use.

» As prompted by the dialog box that appears, enter the text you wish to appear as WordArt and if required, make changes to the font or size or put the text in bold type or italics.

* Confirm the text by clicking **OK**.

*The WordArt object is inserted in the slide and appears with selection handles around it. The **WordArt** toolbar also appears.*

* Use the tools on the **WordArt** toolbar to modify the object:

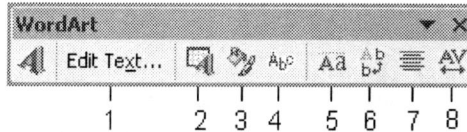

1. changes the inserted text.

2. lets you choose another WordArt effect.

3. modifies the colours of the Word-Art object.

4. lets you choose another shape for your WordArt.

5. gives all the letters the same height.

6. presents the object's text vertically.

7. lets you choose the horizontal alignment of the text.

8. lets you choose how much space to put between the characters.

10 • Resizing an object

Resizing an object approximately

* Select the object you wish to resize.

* Point to one of its sizing handles and check that the mouse pointer takes the shape of a double arrow; for a diagram, the mouse pointer appears as a sizing handle.

* Drag to resize the object.

If you drag one of the handles at the corner of the selection frame, the object's proportions will be preserved.

CREATING AND MODIFYING OBJECTS
Lesson 4.1: Drawing objects

Resizing an object precisely

* Select the object concerned.
* Open the **Format** menu and choose the option corresponding to the object.
* Activate the **Size** tab.

  You cannot use this technique to resize a table.

* Enter the object's new dimensions.

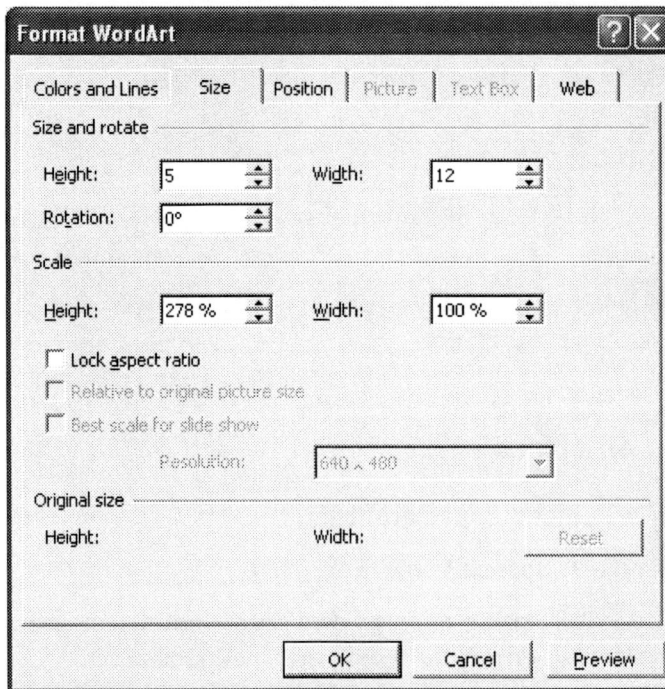

In the **Size and rotate** frame, give a **Height** and/or **Width** in centimetres. The **Height** and **Width** boxes in the **Scale** frame can be used to enter percentages of the object's current size.

* Click **OK**.

11 ▪ Creating a text box

▪ Go to the slide in which you wish to create a text box.

▪ **Insert - Text Box** or 🔲

On the workspace, the mouse pointer becomes a fine black arrow, pointing downwards.

▪ If you know how wide you want your text to be, draw the box outline by dragging the mouse: the width of the box is important, but not its height.
If you do not know what width to use, click the place where you wish to start entering text.

An insertion point appears in a hatched border.

▪ Enter the text.

▪ Press Esc when you have finished.

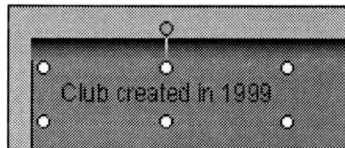

▪ If the size of the text box is unsuitable, resize the object or use the options under the **Text Box** tab in the **Format Text Box** dialog box (**Format - Text Box**).

12 ▪ Applying a border to an object

You can draw border lines around objects such as placeholders, pictures, text boxes, charts, organization charts or diagrams.

▪ Select or click in the object to which you wish to apply a border.

▪ Using the list on the 🖊 tool button on the **Drawing** toolbar, choose the line colour for the border.

Eight colours are offered, linked to the slide's colour scheme; you can select the **More Line Colors** option to choose a different colour. The **Patterned Lines** option opens a dialog box of the same name, in which you can choose a patterned line for your border.

※ Click the ▦ tool button on the **Drawing** toolbar in order to choose the line style and width for the border.

※ Click the ▦ tool button on the **Drawing** toolbar to choose a dashed line style.

📄 You can also open the **Format** menu and choose the option that corresponds to the object, then click the **Colors and Lines** tab. Use the **Color, Style, Dashed** and **Weight** lists to define the border.

To delete a border, open the list on the 🖊 tool button and choose **No Line**.

🔍 You can use the same techniques to change the outline of an AutoShape or any other drawing made with the **Drawing** toolbar (such as a line, an arrow, a rectangle or an oval).

13 ▪ Applying a background colour/fill to an object

▪ Click the object whose background you wish to fill with a colour, pattern, texture etc.

▪ Open the [icon] ▾ list on the **Drawing** toolbar.

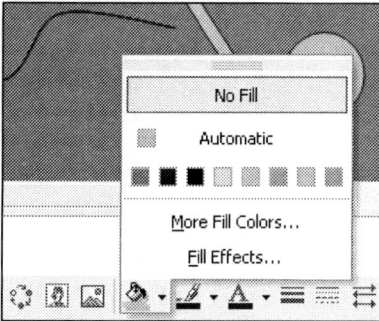

*The **Automatic** option retrieves the object's original background.*

▪ To change the object's background, click one of the colours in the list. If none of these colours is suitable, click the **More Fill Colors** option. Under the **Standard** tab, click the required colour or use the **Custom** page to create your own colour. Click **OK**.

▪ To fill the object with a fill effect or picture, click the **Fill Effects** option and do one of the following:

- to use a gradient, click the **Gradient** tab and select the shading type in the **Colors** frame. Adjust the colour **Transparency**, if required, then choose one of the **Shading styles** and a **Variant**, to determine the gradient's direction. Click **OK**.

- to use a texture, click the **Texture** tab and select the required type of texture; click **OK**.

- to use a pattern, click the **Pattern** tab, choose one of the available patterns then define the **Foreground** and **Background** colours and click **OK**.

- to use a picture as the background fill, click the **Picture** tab, then click the **Select Picture** button. Browse to find the required image file, click the **Insert** button then click **OK** in the **Fill Effects** dialog box.

CREATING AND MODIFYING OBJECTS
Exercise 4.1: Drawing objects

Below you can see **Practice Exercise** 4.1. This exercise is made up of 13 steps. If you do not know how to do one of the steps, go back to the title that corresponds to that particular lesson. When you have finished, you can check your work by reading the **Solution** that follows.

Steps that are likely to be tested during the MOUS exam are marked with this symbol: ⊞. However, it is a good idea to complete the whole exercise to ensure you have understood everything covered in the lesson.

☞ **Practice Exercise 4.1**

*To work on exercise 4.1, you should open the **4-1 Pastimes.ppt** presentation, which is in the **MOUS PowerPoint 2002** folder.*

⊞ 1. Beneath the **Westport Arts and Crafts Centre** title on the first slide, draw a rectangle, halfway between the text and the bottom edge of the slide. This rectangle must be about the same size as the one at the top left of the slide.

⊞ 2. On the first slide, draw an AutoShape using the **Donut** shape type (in the **Basic Shapes** category). Draw this shape at the right-hand end of the rectangle you drew in the previous step.

3. Select the rectangle at the top left of the title slide (the rectangle that was already in the presentation).

4. Delete the rectangle you just selected.

5. If necessary, move the donut shape and/or the rectangle on the first slide so the two objects appear like this:

CRAFTS CENTRE

Now duplicate these objects.

6. Group the donut and rectangle that you just created by duplication.

7. Move the object group you just created so it is aligned vertically with the other donut/rectangle shape. Next, rotate the donut/rectangle shape group until all these drawing objects resemble a pair of scissors.

8. On the first slide, make a freehand drawing to draw the curved line shown below:

9. On the first slide, insert a WordArt object, choosing the effect on the fourth row of the third column in the **WordArt Gallery** dialog box and enter the text **Be creative!**
Change the shape of the WordArt object, applying a **Wave1** shape type (this is the shape in the third row, fifth column in the list of shapes).

10. Resize the WordArt object you created so it is **5 cm** (or 2 inches) high and **12 cm** (or 5 inches) wide. Move the object so it is directly above the **Westport Arts and Crafts Centre** title.

11. At the top left of the first slide, draw a text box and in it, enter the text **Club created in 1999**.

12. Around the text box you just created, apply a border **3 pt** wide, with a double black line.

13. To the text box you have just created, apply a background gradient, using the **Wheat** style of **Preset** gradient. Choose a **Diagonal up** shading style, using the first variant.
Save and close the presentation.

If you want to put what you have learnt into practice on a real document, you can work on summary exercise 4 for the CREATING AND MODIFYING OBJECTS section, that you can find at the end of this book.

CREATING AND MODIFYING OBJECTS
Exercise 4.1: Drawing objects

It is often possible to perform a task in several different ways, but here only the easiest solution is presented. You can go back to the corresponding lesson if you want to see other techniques you could use.

Solution to Exercise 4.1

1. To draw a rectangle as described in step 1, click the ▢ tool button on the **Drawing** toolbar. Place the insertion point halfway between the text and the bottom edge of the slide, under the word **CENTRE**, and drag to draw the rectangle. Aim to make your rectangle the same size as the one at the top left corner of the slide.

2. To draw an AutoShape using the Donut shape type (in the **Basic Shapes** category), open the **AutoShapes** list on the **Drawing** toolbar and drag the pointer to the **Basic Shapes** category. Click the shape called **Donut** (remember that if you point, the shape names appear in a ScreenTip). Point to the right-hand end of the rectangle you drew in step 1 and click to insert an AutoShape of predefined size.

3. To select the rectangle at the top left of the title slide (the rectangle that was already in the presentation), point to the rectangle then click it.

4. To delete the rectangle you just selected, press the Del key.

5. To move the donut and/or rectangle so they resemble the illustration in step 5, click the rectangle to select it, and re-position it, if it was incorrectly positioned. Click the donut shape and drag it to move it on to the right end of the rectangle.

   To duplicate the two objects, select them by clicking one, holding down Shift and clicking the second one then use the **Edit - Duplicate** command.

6. To group the two objects you just created by duplication, make sure they are both selected, open the **Draw** list on the **Drawing** toolbar and click the **Group** option.

7. To move the object group you just created so it is aligned vertically with the other donut/rectangle shape, select the group, if necessary, and drag it towards the left.

   To rotate the donut/rectangle shape group until all these drawing objects form a pair of scissors, point to the object group's rotation handle (the green handle) and rotate the group clockwise until the drawing resembles a pair of scissors.

8. To draw the freehand curve illustrated in step 8, open the **AutoShapes** list on the **Drawing** toolbar and point to the **Lines** category. Click the tool button. Make a succession of clicks, clicking each time you wish to make a summit on the curve and end the line with a double-click.

9. To insert a WordArt object into the first slide, click the tool button on the **Drawing** toolbar. In the **WordArt Gallery** dialog box, click the effect on the fourth row in the third column then click **OK**. Enter the text **Be creative!** Then click **OK** to confirm.

   To change the shape of the WordArt object, click the tool button on the **WordArt** toolbar and in the list that opens, click the effect on the third row of the fifth column, called **Wave1**.

10. To resize the WordArt object so it is 5 cm high and 12 cm wide, select the object if necessary, and use **Format - WordArt**. Click the **Size** tab and in the **Height** box, enter **5** (or **2** if your unit of measurement is inches) then in the **Width** box, enter **12** (or **5** if your unit of measurement is inches) then click **OK**.

    Drag the object until it is directly above the **Westport Arts and Crafts Centre** title.

11. To draw a text box, click the tool button on the **Drawing** toolbar, and click near the top left corner of the first slide. Enter this text: **Club created in 1999** then press Esc. If you wish, deselect the box by pressing Esc again.

12. To put a border around the text box, click inside it to select it. Open the list on the ![tool button] tool button on the **Drawing** toolbar and choose the black colour. Next, click the ![tool button] tool button and choose the **3 pt** double line.

13. To apply a background to the text box, using the "Wheat" preset gradient, click in the text box to select it, if necessary. Open the list on the ![tool button] tool button on the **Drawing** toolbar and click the **Fill Effects** option. In the **Gradient** tab, activate the **Preset** option then open the drop-down **Preset colors** list and choose the effect called **Wheat**. Leave the current **Transparency** and go to the **Shading styles** frame and choose the **Diagonal up** option. Click the top left of the **Variants** and click **OK** to confirm.

    To save and close the presentation, use **File - Close** and click **Yes** when PowerPoint asks you if you want to save the presentation.

CREATING AND MODIFYING OBJECTS
Lesson 4.2: Tables

1 ▪ Creating a table

* Go to the slide in which you want to insert your table.

* Use **Insert - Table** or if your slide contains a placeholder designed to hold tables, charts, pictures etc. (this depends on the layout used), click the **Insert Table** tool button at the centre of the placeholder.

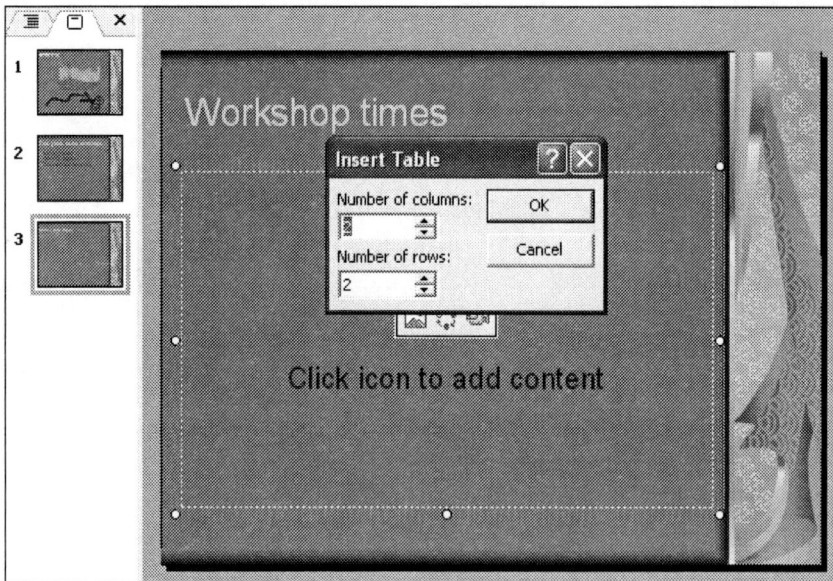

* Give the required **Number of columns** and **Number of rows**.

* Click **OK**.

   *PowerPoint creates the table outline and opens the **Tables and Borders** toolbar.*

* Enter the contents of your table either by clicking in the different cells or by using the following keys:

⇥	to move to the next cell to the right.
Shift ⇥	to move to the previous cell to the left.

⬇   to move to the next cell below.

⬆   to move to the previous cell above.

📑 *A table cannot contain more than 25 rows or columns.*

To insert a tab in a cell, you can press the `Ctrl` `⇥` *keys.*

🔍 *You can also insert a table by clicking the* ⬜ *tool button on the* ***Standard*** *toolbar and then dragging to create the required number of rows and columns for the table.*

2 ▪ Selecting parts of a table

▪ To select a cell, click inside the cell (the pointer takes the shape of a capital "i") or use the keys `⇥` or `Shift` `⇥`. To select several cells, drag over them.

▪ To select a column, position the pointer above the column (the pointer takes the shape of a black downward-pointing arrow); when you see this black arrow, click.
or
Click one of the cells in the column in question then click the **Table** button on the **Tables and Borders** toolbar and select the **Select Column** option.

▪ To select a row, activate a cell in the row you require, click the **Table** button on the **Tables and Borders** toolbar then click the **Select Row** option.

▪ To select the table, click it then click the **Table** button on the **Tables and Borders** toolbar then choose the **Select Table** option.

📑 *You can also select the first cell you require, hold down the* `Shift` *key and click the last cell you wish to select, or drag over the group of cells in question.*

3 ▪ Merging cells

This action combines several cells into a single cell.

▪ Select the cells you wish to merge.

▪ Click the ⊞ tool button on the **Tables and Borders** toolbar.
or

Use the ⟨⟩ tool button on the **Tables and Borders** toolbar. To do this, click the tool button (the pointer takes the form of an eraser) then drag along the vertical line between the cells you want to merge. Click ⟨⟩ again to deactivate it.

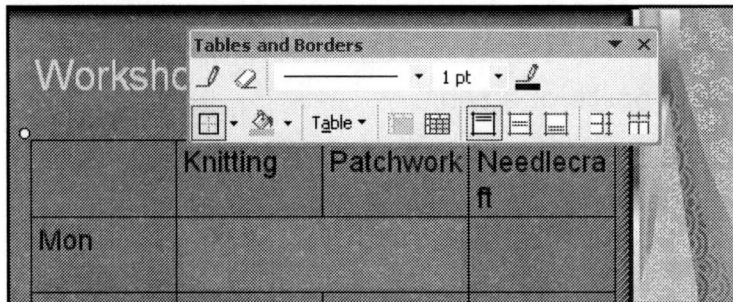

	Knitting	Patchwork	Needlecraft
Mon			

4 ▪ Splitting a cell

This technique divides a cell in two.

▪ Click the cell you want to split.

▪ Click the ⊞ tool button on the **Tables and Borders** toolbar to make a vertical split.
or

Use the ✎ tool button on the **Tables and Borders** toolbar: drag horizontally, vertically or obliquely through the cell to split it in the required way. Click the tool again to deactivate it.

▥5 ▪ Changing the vertical alignment of cell contents

▫ Select the cell(s) concerned.

▫ On the **Tables and Borders** toolbar, click the appropriate tool button:

to align the text at the top of the cell.

to centre the text vertically in the cell.

to align the text at the bottom of the cell.

*You can also choose **Format - Table - Text Box** tab and define the vertical and/or horizontal alignment of text, using the **Text alignment** list.*

To modify the horizontal alignment of text in cells, proceed as if you were aligning ordinary paragraphs.

▥6 ▪ Modifying the width of a column/the height of a row

▫ Point to the vertical line to the right of the column you wish to modify or the horizontal line underneath a row.

The pointer takes the shape of a black double-headed arrow.

▫ Drag to the required position.

*You can also select a group of rows and click on the **Tables and Borders** toolbar to give all the selected rows the same height or select a group of columns and click to give them all the same width.*

You can also double-click the vertical line to the right of a column to make the column adjust to fit its contents.

CREATING AND MODIFYING OBJECTS
Lesson 4.2: Tables

7 ▪ Inserting a row/a column

* Select a cell in the column or row next to which you want to insert a new column or row.

* Click the **Table** button on the **Tables and Borders** toolbar, then click one of the options proposed depending on where exactly you want to insert the new column or row.

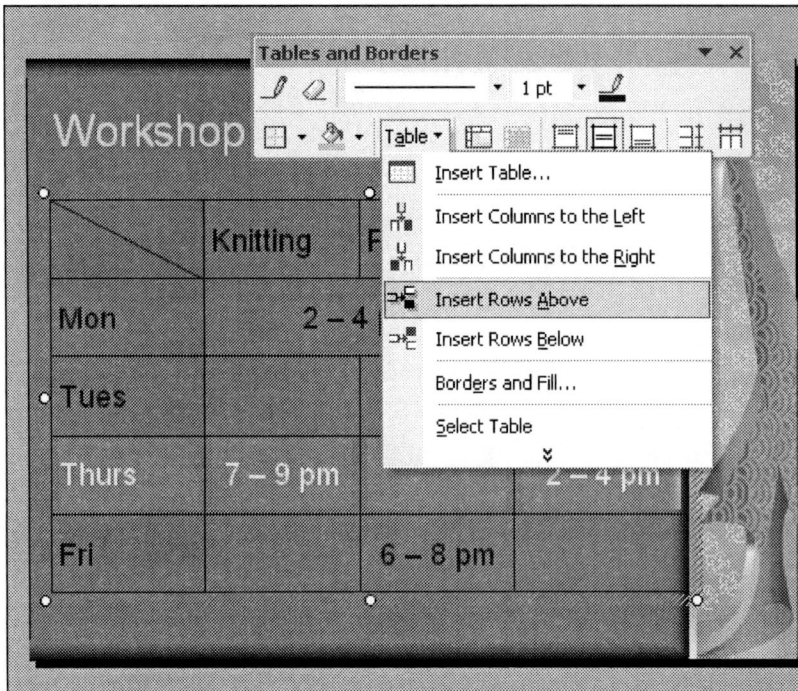

8 ▪ Deleting a row/a column

* Click one of the cells in the row or column you wish to delete.

* Click the **Table** button and choose the **Delete Columns** or **Delete Rows** option.

9 ▪ Modifying cell borders in a table

▪ Select the cells concerned or the entire table.

▪ Use:

| ─────────── ▾ | to choose a line style.

| 1 pt ▾ | to choose a line width.

| 🖊 | to select a colour for the line.

▪ Open the list on the [▢ ▾] tool button (on the **Tables and Borders** toolbar) and select the type of border you wish to apply: **Inside Borders**, **Outside Borders**, a **Left Border** and so on (these names appear in a ScreenTip as you point to each border type).

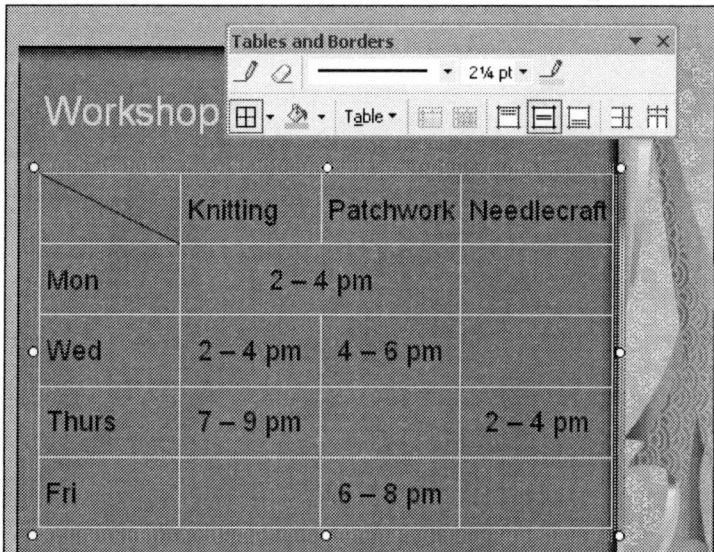

Workshop	Knitting	Patchwork	Needlecraft
Mon	2 – 4 pm		
Wed	2 – 4 pm	4 – 6 pm	
Thurs	7 – 9 pm		2 – 4 pm
Fri		6 – 8 pm	

▪ If the [🖊] tool button activates automatically, click it to deactivate it.

📄 *You can also use the options in **Format - Table - Borders** tab or use the **Borders and Fill** option in the list on the **Table** button (on the **Tables and Borders** toolbar).*

🖳10 ▪ Applying a colour or pattern to cells

▪ Select the cell(s) concerned or the entire table.

▪ Open the list on the [🖌 ▾] tool button and choose a colour from the eight basic colours.
or
Click the **More Fill Colors** option and choose your own colour from the options under the **Standard** and **Custom** tabs.
or
Click the **Fill Effects** option to choose a texture, pattern, picture or gradient to fill the cell.

You can also use the options in **Format - Table - Fill** tab or use the **Borders and Fill** option in the list on the **Table** button (on the **Tables and Borders** toolbar).

Below you can see **Practice Exercise** 4.2. This exercise is made up of 10 steps. If you do not know how to do one of the steps, go back to the title that corresponds to that particular lesson. When you have finished, you can check your work by reading the **Solution** that follows.

Steps that are likely to be tested during the MOUS exam are marked with this symbol: ▦. However, it is a good idea to complete the whole exercise to ensure you have understood everything covered in the lesson.

☞ Practice Exercise 4.2

To work on exercise 4.2, you should open the **4-2 Pastimes.ppt** presentation, which is in the **MOUS PowerPoint 2002** folder.

▦ 1. Activate the last slide and insert a table containing **4** columns and **5** rows. In it, enter the following text (do not worry about its layout for the time being):

	Knitting	Patchwork	Needlecraft
Mon			
Tues			
Thurs			
Fri			

Workshop times

2. Select the second and third cells on the second row.

3. Make sure that the second and third cells on the second row are selected then merge them. Next, enter more details into the table, as shown below:

	Knitting	Patchwork	Needlecraft
Mon	2 – 4 pm		
Tues			3.30 – 5 pm
Thurs	7 – 9 pm		2 – 4 pm
Fri		6 – 8 pm	

4. Split the first cell in the table with an oblique line, as seen here:

	Knitting	Patchwork	Needlecraft
Mon	2 – 4 pm		

5. Vertically centre the contents of all the cells in the table. Next, horizontally centre all the cells except those in the first row and the first column.

6. Make the last column adjust to fit the width of its contents.

7. Insert a row before the **Thurs** row. In the first cell of this new row, type **Wed** then **2 – 4 pm** and **4 – 6 pm** in the next two cells.

8. Delete the **Tues** row.

9. Apply a yellow border, **2¼ pt** wide, to all the cells in the table.

10. In all the cells of the table containing times, apply a green background colour. Save and close the presentation.

If you want to put what you have learnt into practice on a real document, you can work on summary exercise 4 for the CREATING AND MODIFYING OBJECTS section, that you can find at the end of this book.

CREATING AND MODIFYING OBJECTS
Exercise 4.2: Tables

It is often possible to perform a task in several different ways, but here only the easiest solution is presented. You can go back to the corresponding lesson if you want to see other techniques you could use.

Solution to Exercise 4.2

1. To activate the last slide in the presentation, click its thumbnail in the **Slides** tab on the left of the screen. To create a table containing 4 columns and 5 rows, use the **Insert - Table** command. Enter **4** in the **Number of columns** box and **5** in the **Number of rows** box. Click **OK** to insert the table. Click each cell concerned and enter the text shown in step 1.

2. To select the second and third cells on the second row, position the mouse pointer on the second cell in this row then drag over this cell and the third cell. When both cells appear highlighted, release the mouse button.

3. Make sure the second and third cells on the second row are selected (if not, select them). To merge them, click the ⊞ tool button on the **Tables and Borders** toolbar.

   Enter the contents of the table as shown in step 3 of the exercise.

4. To split the first cell in the table with an oblique line, click the ✏ tool button on the **Tables and Borders** toolbar. Point to the top left corner of the first cell in the table then drag to draw a dotted line from this corner to the bottom right corner of the same cell. When the line is drawn, release the mouse button. Click the ✏ tool button again to deactivate it.

5. To vertically centre the contents of all the cells in the table, click any cell, select the table by clicking the **Table** button on the **Tables and Borders** toolbar and choose the **Select Table** option. Next, click the ⊟ tool button on the **Tables and Borders** toolbar.

174

To centre horizontally all the cells except those in the first row and the first column, point to the second cell in the second row of the table and drag down to the right, so as to select all the cells except those in the first row and column. Click the ▤ tool button on the **Formatting** toolbar.

6. To make the last column adjust to fit the width of its contents, point to the vertical line to the right of the column and double-click.

7. To insert a row before the "Thurs" row, click a cell in the **Thurs** row, click the **Table** button on the **Tables and Borders** toolbar and choose the **Insert Rows Above** option.

   Click the first cell of this new row and type **Wed**, then press ⇥ and type **2 – 4 pm** ⇥ **4 – 6 pm**.

8. To delete the "Tues" row, click any cell in this row, click the **Table** button on the **Tables and Borders** toolbar and choose the **Delete Rows** option.

9. To apply a yellow border, 2 ¼ pt wide, to all the cells in the table, start by selecting the table: click a cell, then click the **Table** button on the **Tables and Borders** toolbar and choose the **Select Table** option. Open the list on the ▤ 1 pt ▾ tool button and choose the **2¼ pt** option. Click the ▤ tool button and choose the yellow colour then open the list on the ▤ ▾ tool button and select the ▤ (**All Borders**) option. If necessary, click the ▤ tool button to deactivate it (it may have been activated automatically).

10. To apply a green background to all the cells in the table that contain times, click the first cell concerned (that contains the text **2 – 4 pm**). Open the list on the ▤ ▾ tool button then click the colour green; continue like this, clicking each cell concerned and applying the colour by clicking the ▤ ▾ tool button.

    To save and close the presentation, use **File - Close** and click **Yes** when PowerPoint asks you if you want to save the presentation.

CREATING AND MODIFYING OBJECTS
Lesson 4.3: Multimedia objects/pictures and charts

1 ▪ Inserting a Clip Art picture

- Display the slide in which you want to insert your Clip Art picture.

- Open the **Insert Clip Art** task pane or use:

Insert - Picture - Clip Art or

*This tool button can be found on the **Drawing** toolbar and also in content placeholders, depending on your slide's layout. If you click the button in a content placeholder, it opens the **Select Picture** dialog box, and you can choose from or search in all the available clip art pictures. If you use the **Insert** command, the **Insert Clip Art** task pane opens automatically.*

- If the **Add Clips to Organizer** dialog box appears, you should click **Now** if you want the Organizer to catalogue all the multimedia files on your hard disk, or click **Later** if you do not want to do that just now.

- In the **Search text** box, enter a word or phrase to describe the type of picture you require: to choose from the entire range of Clip Art pictures, leave this text box empty.

The Clip Art pictures are divided into different collections, according to predefined keywords that are associated with them.

- To limit the search to specific collections within the multimedia library, open the **Search in** list.

By default, the multimedia library contains three sets of collections: **My Collections, Office Collections and Web Collections**. Clip Art pictures are stored in **Office Collections**.

- To expand a set of collections, click the plus (+) sign that appears to the left of its name. To collapse a set of collections, click its minus (-) sign.

  When you expand the **Office Collections**, the names of its individual collections appear. Each of these collections contains a specific type of picture.

- Click the check box once to select the corresponding category: click twice to select that category and all its subcategories. Click a third time to deselect that category but keep the selected subcategories selected and click a fourth time to deselect all the subcategories.

- Press ⬅ or click the **Search in** text box to close the list.

- If necessary, specify the type of files you are looking for, using the **Results should be** list. You can limit the search to **Clip Art**, **Photographs**, **Movies** and/or **Sounds**.

  By default, PowerPoint searches for **Clip Art**.

- Click the **Search** button to start the search.

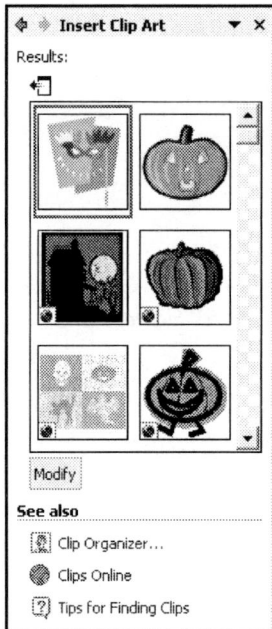

The **Results** frame shows the corresponding pictures that are found.

Clips that have a small globe symbol in their bottom left corner are clips that were found on the Web.

- If necessary, click the [⬜] button to enlarge the **Results** frame.
- Click the required picture to insert it into the slide.

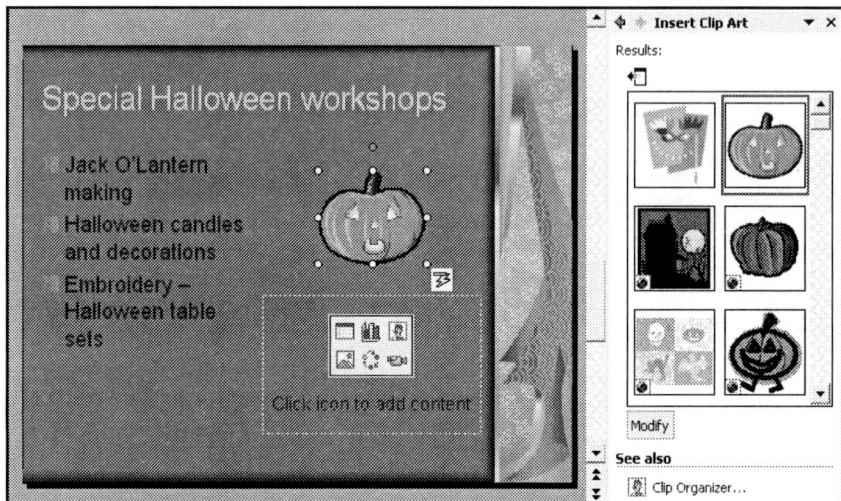

*The picture appears in the middle of the slide or within the content placeholder, if you are using one. The **Picture** toolbar now appears too.*

*The **Automatic Layout Options** button* *may appear next to the inserted picture. If you click it to open its list, you can **Undo Automatic Layout** or **Stop Automatic Layout of Inserted Objects**.*

- To start another search, click the **Modify** button under the **Results** frame and specify other search criteria.

- If you wish, you can edit a picture. Open the **Picture** toolbar if necessary (**View - Toolbars - Picture**), click the picture you wish to modify then use the tool buttons on the **Picture** toolbar:

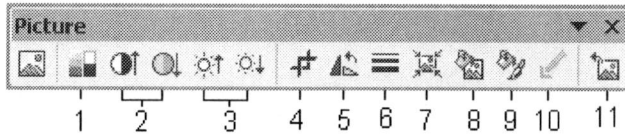

1. to display the picture in **Gray-scale**, **Black & White**, and/or **Washout** (like a watermark).

2. to increase or decrease the contrast.

3. to increase or decrease the brightness.

4. to crop the image.

5. to rotate the picture 90 degrees to the left.

6. to choose a line to frame the picture.

7. to compress the picture to reduce the file size.

8. to change the picture's colours.

9. opens the **Format Picture** dialog box.

10. to make certain colours in the picture transparent (this is not available for all clip art).

11. retrieves the original picture.

If you wish to open the **Clip Organizer** dialog box, click the **Clip Organizer** link at the bottom of the **Insert Clip Art** task pane.

The **Clips Online** link takes you to a Microsoft Web site, where you can search for extra multimedia files.

⊞2 ▪ Inserting one or more picture files

▪ Activate the slide concerned.

▪ **Insert - Picture - From File** or 🖼

▪ Go to the drive and/or folder that contains the picture file you wish to insert.

In the dialog box, the list on the ▦▾ tool button can change the view of the file list, so you can see the picture files as **Large Icons**, as **Small Icons**, as a **List**, with **Details**, with a **Preview** or as **Thumbnails**.

▪ Double-click the picture you want to insert,
or
to insert several pictures at once, hold down the [Shift] key as you click each picture then click the **Insert** button.

The picture can appear in the middle of the slide or in the content placeholder intended for this type of object, as shown here.

3 ▪ Compressing pictures

Presentations containing pictures can have large file sizes; compressing the pictures that the slides contain can reduce this.

▪ If you do not want to compress all the pictures in your presentation, select the picture(s) concerned.

▪ Click the [▣] tool button on the **Picture** toolbar.

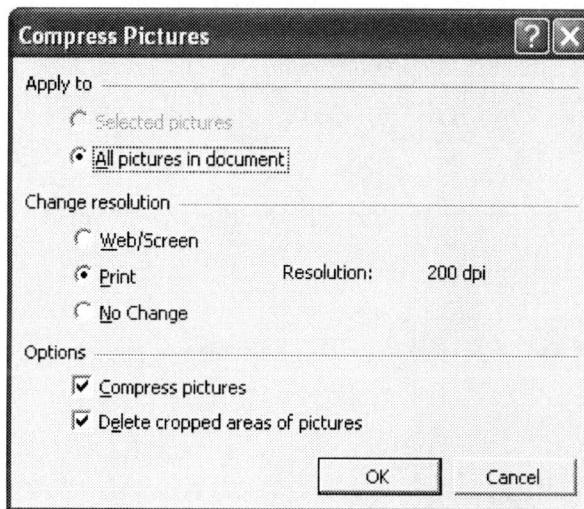

▪ Specify whether you want to compress the **Selected pictures** or **All pictures in document**.

▪ Choose the **Web/Screen** option to apply a resolution of 96 dpi (dots per inch) or the **Print** option to apply a resolution of 200 dpi (this will compress the pictures less than with the former option).

▪ Check that the **Compress pictures** option is active.

▪ The **Delete cropped areas of pictures** option is active by default; this will remove any parts of the picture that are trimmed. You can deactivate it if you want to keep these cropped parts.

▪ Click **OK**.

PowerPoint warns you that compressing your pictures may reduce their quality.

▪ Click the **Apply** button.

📄 *You can also compress a picture with* **Format - Picture - Picture** *tab -* **Compress** *button.*

📖4 ▪ Inserting a sound

You can insert sounds that PowerPoint will play during your slide show.

▪ Activate the slide in which you want to insert the sound object.

Inserting a sound from the Clip Organizer

▪ **Insert - Movies and Sounds - Sound from Clip Organizer**

*The **Insert Clip Art** task pane opens and displays the results of PowerPoint's search in the Clip Organizer. The **Modify** button allows you to run a new search in the Clip Organizer according to specific criteria.*

* Click the sound you want to insert.

A message appears asking you how you want your sound to play:

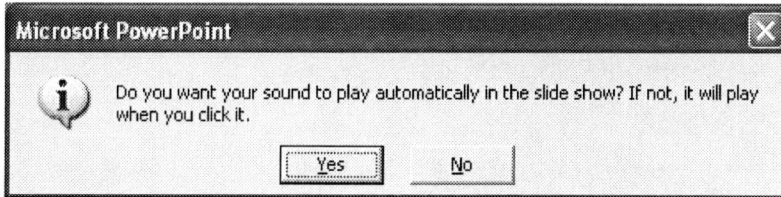

Microsoft PowerPoint

Do you want your sound to play automatically in the slide show? If not, it will play when you click it.

Yes   No

* Click **Yes** if you want your sound to play automatically in a slide show or click **No** if you want to play the sound manually (in which case, you click the sound icon during the slide show).

PowerPoint displays a loudspeaker icon in the middle of the slide to represent the sound.

You can also click the   tool button that appears in a slide with a content placeholder.

Inserting a sound file

* **Insert - Movies and Sounds - Sound from File**

*The **Insert Sound** dialog box opens (this is similar to the **Open** dialog box).*

* Go to the folder that contains the sound file you want to insert.

* Double-click the name of the sound file you want to insert.

* In response to the message asking you how you want your sound to play, click **Yes** if you want your sound to play automatically in a slide show or click **No** if you want to play the sound manually.

Like sounds from the Clip Gallery, inserted sound files are represented by a loudspeaker icon.

Recording a sound

If your computer has a sound card and a microphone, you can record a sound.

- **Insert - Movies and Sounds - Record Sound**

  *The **Record Sound** dialog box opens.*

- Enter the name of your sound.

  *PowerPoint adds the sound to the **Sound** list in the **Slide Transition** task pane and also to the dialog box used to customise animations.*

- Click the  button to start recording.
- Start speaking or start playing the sound you want to record.
- Click the  button to stop the recording.

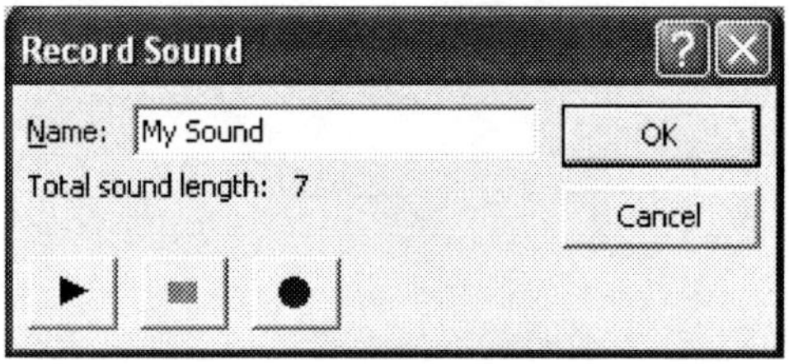

You can click  to listen to what you have recorded.

- Click **OK** to insert the recording into the slide.

Like sounds inserted from the Clip Gallery or from sound files, sounds that you record yourself are also symbolised by a loudspeaker icon.

To hear a recorded sound, click it during the slide show.
The sound is recorded for the active presentation.

Inserting a sound object from an audio CD

- Place the audio CD in the CD-ROM drive.
- **Insert - Movies and Sounds - Play CD Audio Track**

© Editions ENI - All rights reserved

⊛ Activate the **Loop until stopped** check box, if you want your sound to repeat continuously to the end of the slide show.

⊛ In the **Track** boxes, choose the start and end tracks.

To play a single track, enter the same number in both text boxes.

⊛ If necessary, in the **At** text boxes, enter the time within the track (start and/or end) when the sound should start or stop playing.

Movie and Sound Options	? X

Play options
- ☑ Loop until stopped
- ☐ Rewind movie when done playing

Play CD audio track

Start:		End:	
Track:	3	Track:	3
At:	00:00	At:	04:07

Total playing time: 04:07
File: [CD Audio]

OK   Cancel

By default, the start time is fixed at zero and the end time is calculated from the total length of the end track.

⊛ Click **OK**.

⊛ If a message appears concerning how the sound will be played, click **Yes** to play the sound automatically during the slide show, or **No** to play it manually.

A sound object inserted with this technique is represented by a CD symbol.

📄 *To repeat a sound continuously (any type of sound object), click it then use Edit - Sound Object then tick the Loop until stopped option.*

When you insert a sound object, you create simultaneously an animation effect that you can customise if you wish.

🔊 *To listen to a sound in a slide, when you are not in a slide show, double-click the sound icon.*

5 ▪ **Inserting a movie**

Inserting a movie from the Clip Organizer

▪ **Insert - Movies and Sounds - Movie from Clip Organizer**

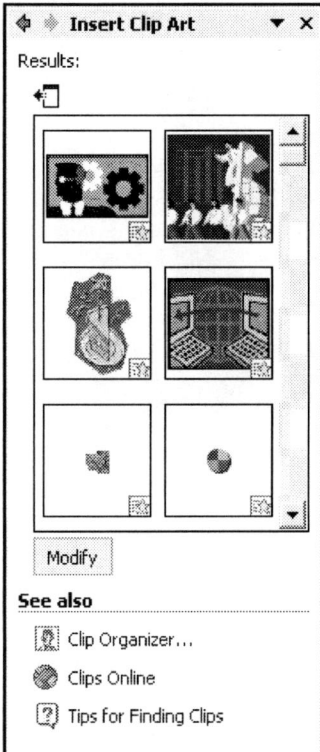

The ***Insert Clip Art*** *task pane opens and displays the results of PowerPoint's search in the Clip Organizer.*

*You can click the **Modify** button to run a new search with specific criteria.*

▪ Click the movie you want to insert.

📄 *Movies play automatically when you run a slide show.*

You can also insert a movie by clicking the 🎞 tool button that appears in a slide with a content placeholder.

Inserting a movie from a video file

■ **Insert - Movies and Sounds - Movie from File**

The *Insert Movie* dialog box opens (this is similar to the *Open* dialog box).

■ Access the folder that contains the movie file you want to insert.

■ Double-click the name of the movie file you want to insert.

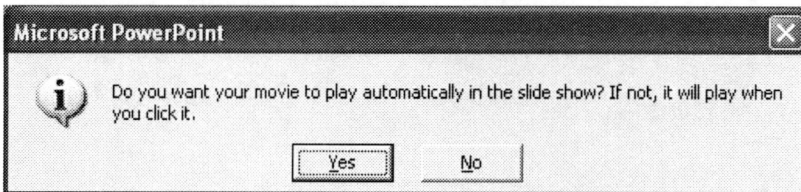

As with sounds, PowerPoint asks you how you want your movie to play.

■ Click **Yes** if you want your movie to play automatically in a slide show or click **No** if you want to play the movie manually. To play it manually, you need to click the icon representing the movie during the slide show.

6 ▪ Creating a chart in a slide

■ Go to the slide in which you want to insert the chart.

■ **Insert - Chart** or 📊

This tool button exists in slides with a content placeholder.

Lesson 4.3: Multimedia objects/pictures and charts

The **Microsoft Graph 2002** *application starts immediately. A worksheet, called* **Datasheet***, appears in the foreground and the corresponding chart is inserted in the slide. The data shown are just examples for the moment. The* **Standard** *and* **Formatting** *toolbars are specific to the* **Microsoft Graph** *application.*

* Enter your data in the datasheet (cf. Below Working with the datasheet).

* Click the [icon] tool button to insert a data table (or remove it if it is currently displayed). A data table displays the chart data in an adjacent worksheet.

   When it is inserted, the data table appears beneath the chart. You can modify its presentation (fonts, fill etc.) by double-clicking it.

* To leave Microsoft Graph 2002, click the slide, outside the placeholder containing the chart.

> Back in the presentation, you may wish to modify your chart: to do this, go to the slide containing the chart in question and double-click the chart.

☐7 ▪ Working with the datasheet

The datasheet allows you to enter all the data that the chart will represent.

Displaying/hiding the datasheet

▪ **View - Datasheet** or ⊞

Moving around and/or selecting items in the datasheet

▪ To move around in the datasheet, you can use the scroll bars or the following keys:

Home   to go to the column before column A.

End   to go the last column containing data.

| Ctrl Home / Ctrl End | to go to the first/last cell containing a value. |
| PgUp / PgDn | to go one screen up/down. |

- To select cells, drag over them or use Shift-clicks.

- To select rows or columns, click the headers concerned or start in a cell in the row/column concerned and press Shift Space to select a row or Ctrl Space to select a column.

- To select all the cells in the datasheet, click the **Select All** button (the top left button at the intersection of the rows and columns) or use Ctrl **A**.

Entering data

- Activate the first cell in the datasheet and type in the data.

- Go to the next cell concerned and type in the next piece of data.

- To modify a cell's contents without clearing it entirely, double-click that cell or click it and press the F2 key.

> *By default, pressing ⏎ activates the next cell down. If this does not occur, you can use **Tools - Options**, click the **Datasheet Options** tab and activate the **Move selection after Enter** option.*
>
> *You can also enter data in the datasheet by pasting in data that you have copied into the clipboard.*

Clearing data and/or formats

- Select the cells whose contents you wish to clear.

- **Edit - Clear**

- Indicate what you want to delete:

  All   to delete both the contents of the selected cells and the formatting applied to them.

  Contents   to delete only the data in the cells.

Formats   to remove the cells' formatting.

Behind the datasheet, the chart reflects the changes you have made to the data.

📄   *The* ⌈Del⌋ *key deletes just the contents of the selected cell(s).*

Inserting rows/columns

▪ Select the row/column before which you wish to insert the new one.

▪ **Insert - Cells** or ⌈Ctrl⌋⌈Shift⌋ **+** (alphanumerical keyboard)

Deleting rows/columns

▪ Select the rows or columns you want to delete.

▪ **Edit - Delete** or ⌈Ctrl⌋ **-** (alphanumerical keyboard)

📄   *Microsoft Graph always shows four categories (columns) by default. If using less than these four, you should always delete this last column or the layout of your chart will be affected.*

Excluding certain rows/columns

It is possible to leave data out of the chart without deleting it from the datasheet.

▪ Select the row(s) or column(s) you wish to exclude.

▪ **Data - Exclude Row/Col**

The data in excluded rows or columns appears in grey and the row/column header appears differently. The chart adjusts to reflect the changes in the datasheet.

📄 *To reintegrate excluded rows or columns, select them and use **Data - Include Row/Col**.*

Formatting numerical values

※ Select the cells whose number formats you wish to change.

※ Depending on your needs, click one of the following tool buttons on the **Formatting** toolbar:

to apply a currency style.

[%] to apply a percentage style; this style multiplies the numbers by 100.

[,] to apply a comma style (thousands separator and two decimal places).

[+.0 .00] to increase the number of decimal places.

[.00 +.0] to decrease the number of decimal places.

» If the style you require does not appear on the **Formatting** toolbar, use the **Format - Number** command, select the appropriate category then double-click the format you wish to apply.

The scale of the chart takes the format of the number values in the first series of the chart.

Changing column width

» Select the columns whose width you wish to change (if you select several columns, they will all adopt the same width).

» Point to the vertical line to the right of the header of the last column selected.

» Drag to change the width or double-click to adjust the column width to the contents.

*You can also use the **Format - Column Width** command.*

If a column is not wide enough to contain a value, the value appears as hash symbols (#).

CREATING AND MODIFYING OBJECTS
Lesson 4.3: Multimedia objects/pictures and charts

8 ▪ Customising a chart

* If necessary, double-click the chart to open it in Microsoft Graph.

* To select a chart object, point to the object, check the name that appears in a ScreenTip then click, or open the **Chart Objects** list on the **Standard** toolbar and click the name of the element you wish to select.

* To select a data point within a series, click the point once to select the series then a second time to select that particular point (be sure not to double-click).

* To select a text object, click the text and press Esc.

Changing the chart type

* **Chart - Chart Type**

* In the **Chart type** list, select the basic category of chart.

196

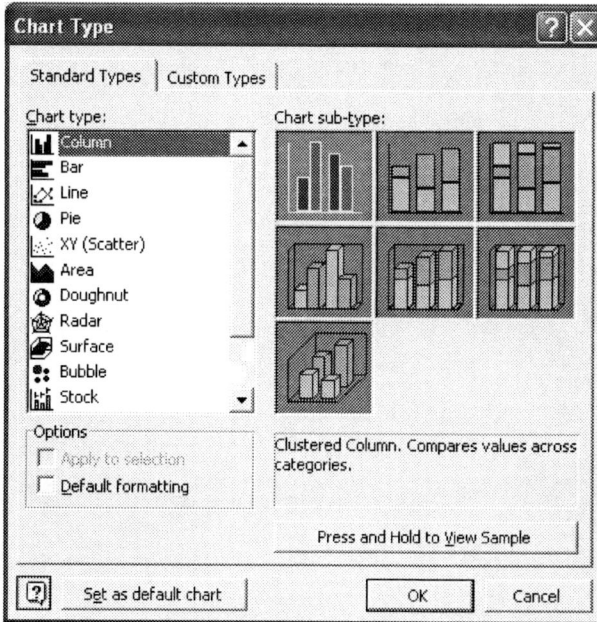

For each category of chart, there is a set of sub-types. The sub-types shown are just examples and are not based on the data within the datasheet.

- To see what your data would look like within a particular sub-type, select the type then hold down the **Press and Hold to View Sample** button.

- In the **Options** frame, check that the **Apply to selection** option is either greyed-out or inactive.

- Double-click the sub-type you want to use.

To change the view of a 3-D chart, use the **Chart - 3-D View** command and change the **Elevation** and/or the **Rotation** of the 3-D chart.

You can also change the chart type using the ◆ list: this list shows the major chart types but does not let you choose a sub-type.

Choosing the position of data series

▫ To make the series appear in the rows, choose:

Data - Series in Rows or ⊞

▫ To make the series appear in the columns, choose:

Data - Series in Columns or ⊞

Adding titles to a chart

▫ **Chart - Chart Options**

▫ Activate the **Titles** tab.

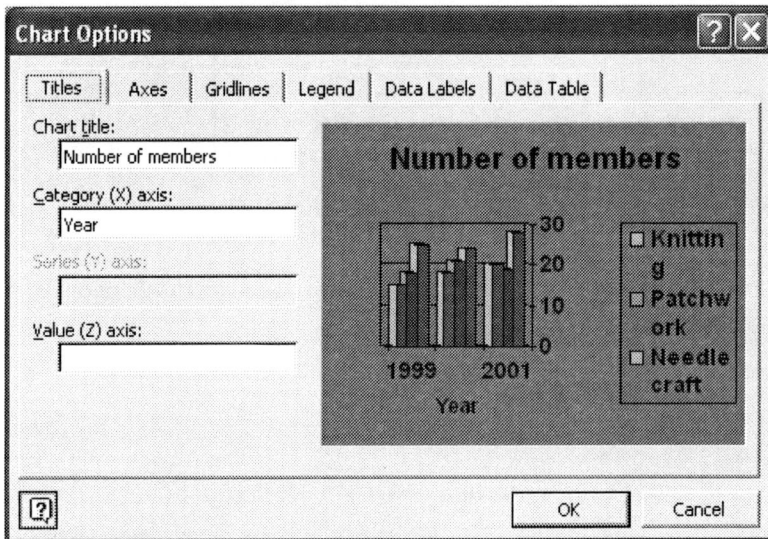

▫ Type the titles in the appropriate text boxes.

▫ Click **OK** to confirm.

You can modify a title by clicking it directly. This technique allows you to use the ↵ key when you want to present a title over several lines.

Below you can see **Practice Exercise** 4.3. This exercise is made up of 8 steps. If you do not know how to do one of the steps, go back to the title that corresponds to that particular lesson. When you have finished, you can check your work by reading the **Solution** that follows.

Steps that are likely to be tested during the MOUS exam are marked with this symbol: ⊞. However, it is a good idea to complete the whole exercise to ensure you have understood everything covered in the lesson.

☞ Practice Exercise 4.3

To work on exercise 4.3, you should open the **4-3 Pastimes.ppt** presentation, which is in the **MOUS PowerPoint 2002** folder.

⊞ 1. Activate the fourth slide in the presentation and to the right of the first paragraph, insert a picture of a pumpkin from the Clip Organizer. Limit your search to clips about **Halloween**.

⊞ 2. On the same slide, insert the picture called **Halloween.gif**, which is in the **MOUS PowerPoint 2002** folder.

3. Compress all the pictures in the presentation.

⊞ 4. On the fourth slide in the presentation, insert the sound file called **Owl.wav**, which is in the **MOUS PowerPoint 2002** folder. Set the sound to play automatically when the slide show starts.

⊞ 5. On the last slide in the presentation, insert the video file called **Child.wmv**, which is in the **MOUS PowerPoint 2002** folder. Set the movie to play automatically.

⊞ 6. On the second slide of the presentation, insert a chart into the content placeholder. Do not leave the Microsoft Graph application.

🪟 7. Enter the following data into the datasheet:

4-3 Pastimes - Datasheet		A	B	C	D	E
		1999	2000	2001	2002	
1	Knitting	15	18	20	21	
2	Patchwork	18	21	19	20	
3	Needlecraft	25	24	28	29	
4						

Exclude the data in column D.

8. Add the title **Number of members** to the chart and put the title **Year** on the category (X) axis. You can now leave the Microsoft Graph application. Save and close the presentation.

If you want to put what you have learnt into practice on a real document, you can work on summary exercise 4 for the CREATING AND MODIFYING OBJECTS section, that you can find at the end of this book.

It is often possible to perform a task in several different ways, but here only the easiest solution is presented. You can go back to the corresponding lesson if you want to see other techniques you could use.

Solution to Exercise 4.3

1. To activate the fourth slide in the presentation, click its thumbnail in the **Slides** tab. To insert a Clip Art picture into the slide, click the ▣ tool button on the **Drawing** toolbar.

   In the **Search text** box, type the word **Halloween** then click the **Search** button.

   Click an image in the **Results** frame that shows a pumpkin.

2. To insert the "Halloween.gif" file from the MOUS PowerPoint 2002 folder, make sure slide 4 is still active, then click the ▣ tool button on the **Drawing** toolbar. Browse to go to the **MOUS PowerPoint 2002** folder then double-click the **Halloween.gif** file.

3. To compress all the pictures in the presentation, display the **Picture** toolbar if necessary (use **View - Toolbars - Picture**) then click the ▣ tool button. Check that the **All pictures in document**, **Print**, **Compress pictures** and **Delete cropped areas of pictures** options are active (if not, tick each check box), click **OK** then click the **Apply** button.

4. To insert the "Owl.wav" file from the MOUS PowerPoint 2002 folder into the fourth slide in the presentation, click the slide thumbnail to activate it. Next, use the **Insert - Movies and Sounds - Sound from File** command. Browse to go to the **MOUS PowerPoint 2002** folder then double-click the **Owl.wav** file. Click **Yes** so the sound plays automatically during the slide show.

5. To insert the "Child.wmv" movie file into the last slide of the presentation, click the last slide on the **Slides** tab then use the **Insert - Movies and Sounds - Movie from File** command. Browse to go to the **MOUS PowerPoint 2002** folder then double-click the **Child.wmv** file. Click the **Yes** button so the movie plays automatically during the slide show.

6. To create a chart on the second slide in the presentation, click that slide's thumbnail in the **Slides** tab. In the content placeholder, click the ▦ tool button.

7. To enter the data described in step 7, click each cell in the datasheet and replace the current data by the new values shown in the exercise.

   To exclude column D, select it by clicking its header then use the **Data - Exclude Row/Col** command.

8. To add the title "Number of members" to the chart and the title "Year" to the category axis, use the **Chart - Chart Options** command. Under the **Titles** tab, in the **Chart title** box, type **Number of members** and in the **Category (X) axis** box, type **Year**. Click **OK**.

   To leave the Microsoft Graph application, click anywhere on the slide outside the chart or datasheet.

   To save and close the presentation, use the **File - Close** command and click **Yes** when PowerPoint prompts you to save the presentation.

SLIDE SHOWS
Lesson 5.1: Working with slide shows

▥1 ▪ Setting up a slide show

When you display the slides of a presentation on screen, this is called a slide show. By default, a slide show is displayed full screen. The presenter has complete control over the running of the slide show and the slides must be scrolled manually.

※ **Slide Show - Set Up Show**

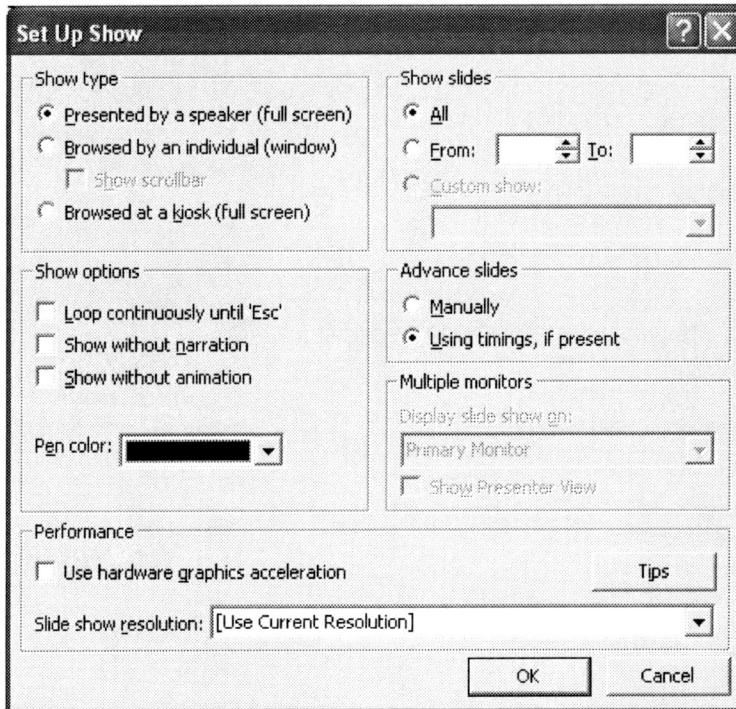

※ In the **Show type** frame, activate the required option:

Presented by a speaker (full screen)	The presenter can scroll through the slides and animations manually or program them to run automatically.

Browsed by an individual (window)	The slide show runs in a normal window with scroll bars (if the **Show scrollbar** option is active). The presenter can scroll the slides but not the animations.
Browsed at a kiosk (full screen)	If the slides are timed, they will play in a loop and users can scroll the slides or animations. They will not be able to modify the presentation (this type of show is generally used for stands or demonstrations). If the slides are not timed, the slide show will stay on the first slide. Once you activate this option PowerPoint activates the **Loop continuously until 'Esc'** option automatically (and it then becomes inaccessible).

⁕ In the **Show slides** frame, tick the **All** option if you want to include all the slides in the presentation in the slide show. If you want to include only part of the presentation, give the starting slide in the **From** box and the end slide in the **To** box.

⁕ If you want a timed slide show to play in a loop until the presenter presses the Esc key, activate the **Loop continuously until 'Esc'** option.

⁕ To run a slide show without any vocal commentary recorded during the presentation, activate the **Show without narration** option.

*If your computer has a sound card, a microphone and loudspeakers, you can record your vocal comments during the slide show, using the **Slide Show - Record Narration** command.*

⁕ To view the slide show as a presentation, without any animation effects, tick the **Show without animation** option.

⁕ Choose the **Pen color**.

The pen is used to make notes during the slide show.

⁕ To run a slide show on several screens (you must first install and configure the material in the **Control Panel**), go to the **Multiple monitors** frame and in the **Display slide show on** list, choose the screen on which you want to see the slide show (for example a projector or a wide screen, instead of on the presenter's screen or a laptop) then activate the **Show Presenter View** option.

※ Click **OK** to close the **Set Up Show** dialog box.

📖2 ▪ **Starting a slide show**

※ **Slide Show - View Show** or 🖥 or F5

*You can also use the **View - Slide Show** command or click the* 🖥 Slide Show *button on certain task panes.*

When you move the mouse, the button containing the slide show options menu appears in the bottom left corner during the slide show: 🖐△.

※ If the slides do not scroll automatically, scroll through them manually (cf. section below).

※ To finish the slide show, you can be in the last slide and ask to see the next slide or, if you are elsewhere, press the Esc key.

※ To start an animation that is not automated, click with the mouse or use one of these keys: Space, →, ↓, **N**, PgDn.

※ To start playing a sound or a movie that does not play automatically, point to the object and make sure that the pointer has taken the shape of a hand, then click.

When you leave the current slide show, you return to the presentation, at the last slide shown.

Slide shows end with a black slide that PowerPoint creates automatically in Slide Show view. If you do not want this black slide to appear use **Tools - Options - View** tab and deactivate the **End with black slide** option.

The button on the tabs pane or the **Slide Show** button on certain task panes start a slide show that begins with the active slide.

ᴨ3 ▪ Scrolling through slides

▪ To go to the next slide, click with the mouse or use one of these keys: **N**, `Space` `→`, `↓`, or `PgDn`.

▪ To go to the previous slide, type **P**, or press `↑`, `←` or `PgUp`.

▪ To return to the first slide, press `Home`; to go to the last slide in the show, press `End`.

▪ To go to a particular slide, enter that slide's number and confirm with `↵`.

If you enter a number that does not exist, you will automatically go to the last slide.

▪ If you know the title of the slide you wish to reach, you can:

  - Move the mouse until the button appears then click it.

  - Drag the pointer to the **Go** option then point to the **By Title** option.

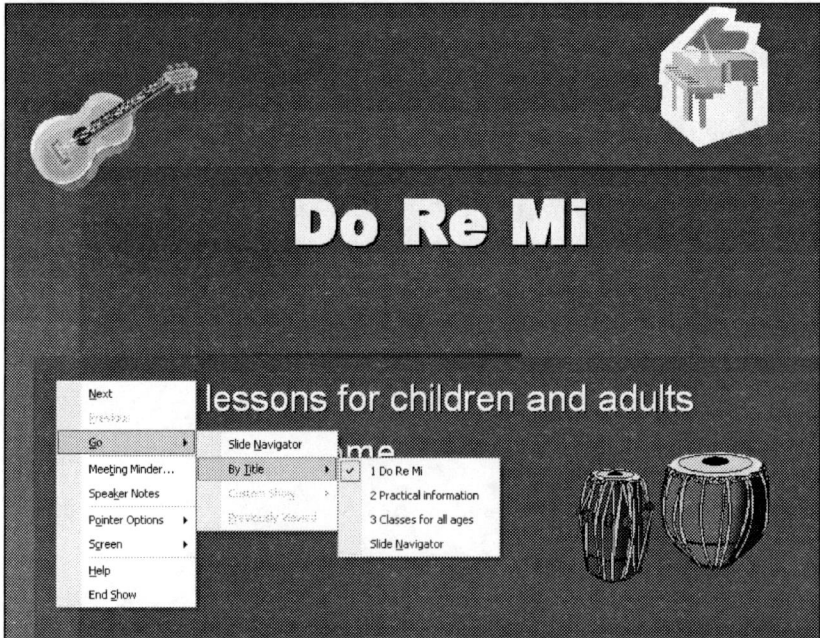

- Click the title of the slide to which you want to go.

 You can also open the slide show options menu by pressing [Shift][F10] or by right-clicking the screen.

4 ▪ Drawing on a slide during a slide show

You can change the mouse pointer into a "pen" that you can then use to make drawings (arrows, circles etc.) on the slides during the slide show.

▪ Start the slide show and let it scroll to the slide on which you want to make notes.

▪ Press [Ctrl] **P** to change the pointer into a pen.

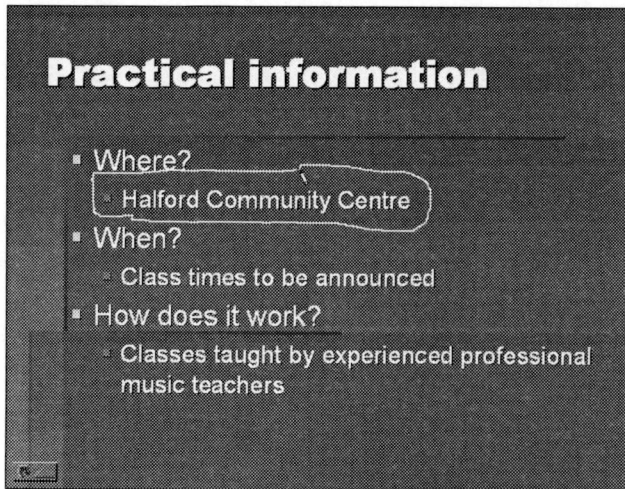

* Drag to make a drawing. If you want to use perfectly horizontal, vertical or diagonal lines you should hold down the [Shift] key as you drag.

* To delete your drawings and keep the pointer as a pen, press the **E** key.

* To make the pen become a pointer again, press [Ctrl] **A**.

> You can change the colour of the pen, using **Slide Show - Set Up Show** and choosing a colour from the **Pen color** list or, if you are in a slide show, click the [button] button, point to **Pointer Options - Pen Color** and choose a colour from the list.

5 ▪ Filling out a notes page during a slide show

This adds notes to the presentation, as you could do in the notes pane in Normal view or in Notes Page view.

* During the slide show, make sure you are in the slide to which you want to add notes.

* Click the [button] button or right-click to display the slide show shortcut menu.

▪ Activate the **Speaker Notes** option.

A dialog box appears: if you have already entered notes for this slide in Notes Page view or in the notes pane, they appear in the box.

▪ Type your notes.

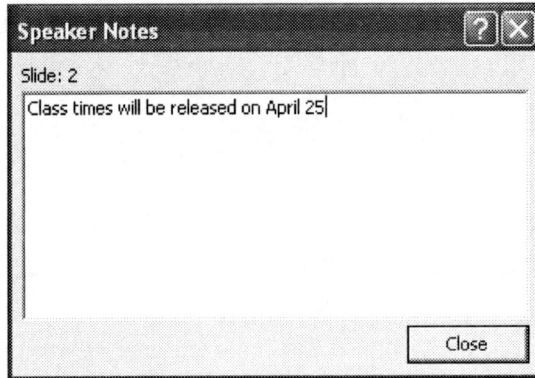

▪ Click **Close**.

📄 *Online meeting participants can also use the **Speaker Notes** dialog box. All online participants will be able to view these notes.*

⊞6 ▪ Defining for how long slides will be displayed

You can scroll slides automatically, with a specific display time for each slide (once the animation effects are finished). There are two ways of doing this: set the timings manually or save the timings as you run the slide show.

Setting slide timings manually

▪ Select the slides whose timings you wish to set.

▪ **Slide Show - Slide Transition** or ⊞ (in **Slide Sorter** view)

*If it was closed, the **Slide Transition** task pane opens at the right hand side of the window.*

» Under **Advance slide**, tick the **Automatically after** check box then enter the amount of time (in seconds) that the selected slides should remain on the screen.

» If you want to keep the option of scrolling the slides manually, leave the **On mouse click** option active.

» If you selected the slides concerned before modifying the options, you do not need to confirm. If you selected nothing, and you wish to apply these timings to the whole presentation, click the **Apply to All Slides** button.

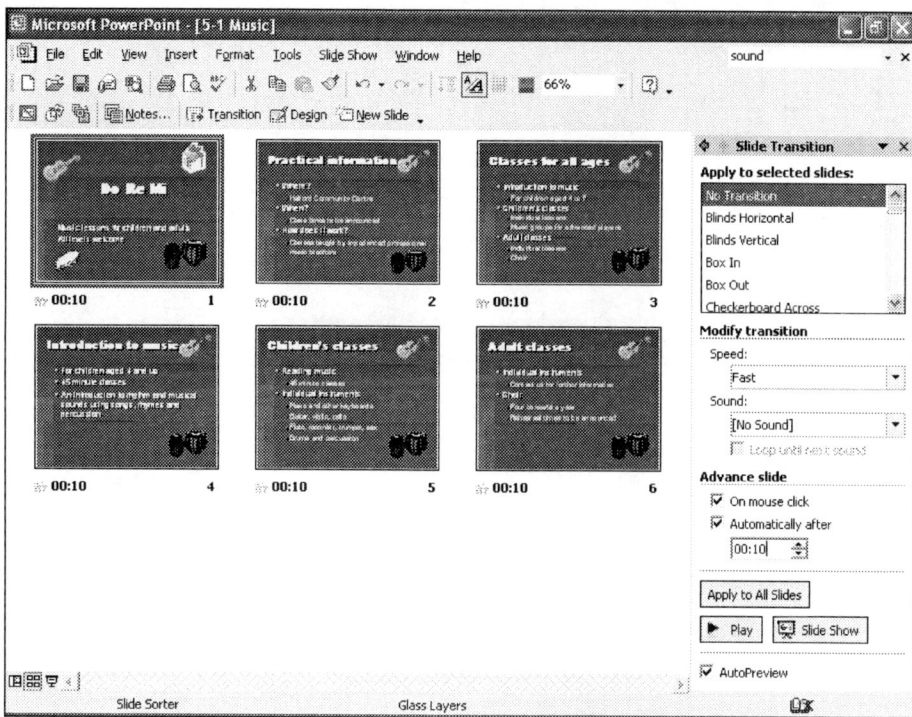

In Slide Sorter view you can see the display time underneath each slide thumbnail.

» Use the **Slide Show - Set Up Show** command and in the **Advance slides** frame, make sure that the **Using timings, if present** option is active.

Running a slide show to record its timings

* If necessary, go to the slide show settings and choose which slides you want to check the timings for (using the **From** and **To** boxes).

* **Slide Show - Rehearse Timings** or [icon] on the **Slide Sorter** toolbar

Rehearsal		▼ ✕
➡ ‖	0:00:05 ↻	0:00:14

*The first slide appears and PowerPoint opens the **Rehearsal** toolbar. The timer starts immediately.*

* Depending on your needs, use the following buttons:

➡	goes to the next slide once enough time has gone by.
‖	pauses the timer; click this button again to restart.
0:00:05	shows the display time for the active slide.
↻	resets the timer for the active slide. The timing restarts automatically afterwards.
0:00:14	shows the total time for the slide show.

* To go to the next slide, you can also enter a specific time (in hh:mm:ss format) in the 0:00:05 text box.

* To stop the timing rehearsal before the end of the slide show you can press Esc or close the **Rehearsal** toolbar by clicking the ✕ button.

At the end of the show a message appears:

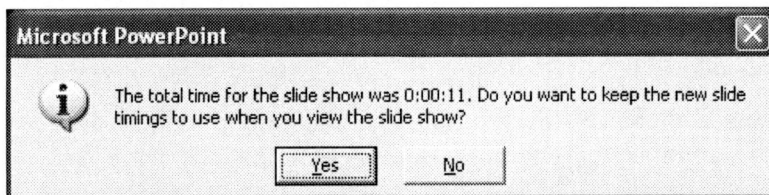

Microsoft PowerPoint	✕
ⓘ The total time for the slide show was 0:00:11. Do you want to keep the new slide timings to use when you view the slide show?	
Yes No	

▪ Click the **Yes** button to accept the new timings.

▥7 ▪ Applying a transition effect to slides

A ***transition*** *is the way in which a slide appears on the screen during a slide show. You can apply transition effects with or without timings.*

▪ Select the slides concerned by the same transition effect.

▪ If it is closed, open the **Slide Transition** task pane with the **Slide Show - Slide Transition** command or by clicking the tool button in **Slide Sorter** view.

▪ In the **Apply to selected slides** list, choose the transition effect you want to apply.

*If the **AutoPreview** check box is active at the bottom of the **Slide Transition** task pane, PowerPoint will provide an immediate preview of the transition effect you choose.*

▪ In the **Modify transition** section, open the **Speed** list and choose one of the options: **Slow**, **Medium** or **Fast**.

▪ If you previously selected the slides concerned, you do not need to confirm. If you made no selection and you want to apply your transition effect to all the slides in the presentation, click the **Apply to All Slides** button on the task pane.

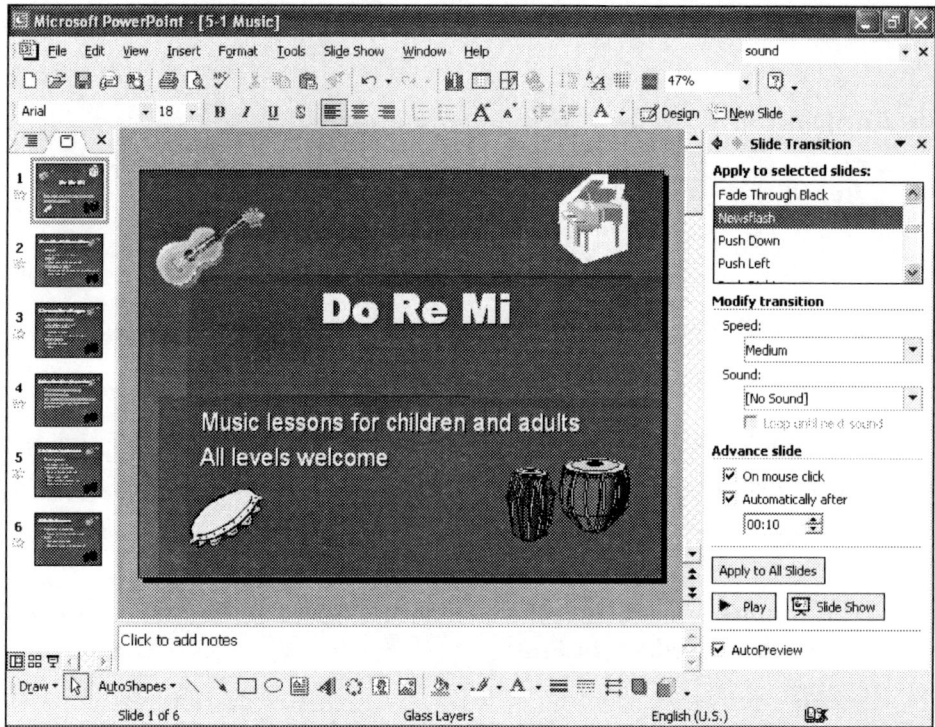

As soon as you apply a transition effect to a slide, this icon ✲ appears next to the thumbnail on the **Slides** tab or under the thumbnail in Slide Sorter view.

If you wish to remove the transition effect applied to a slide, select the slide and choose the **No Transition** option in the **Apply to selected slides** section of the task pane.

To test the effect of the chosen transition again, click the ▶ Play button on the **Slide Transition** task pane or click the ✲ symbol next to the slide thumbnail.

📖8 ▪ Associating a sound with a slide transition

You can associate a sound with the appearance of a slide: this is not necessarily coupled with a visual effect, as sound transitions and visual effects are independent of each other.

▪ Select the slides on which you want to apply the same sound as a transition effect.

▪ If it is closed, open the **Slide Transition** task pane with the **Slide Show - Slide Transition** command or by clicking the 🔳 tool button in **Slide Sorter** view.

▪ In the **Modify transition** section, open the **Sound** list and choose one of the sounds on offer. If the sound you wish to apply is not in the list, click the **Other Sound** option at the end of the list and choose a different sound.

It is possible that the sound effects feature may not be installed. PowerPoint will display a message to tell you this. If this is the case, insert your Office XP or PowerPoint 2002 installation CD and click Yes to install the component.

▪ Activate the **Loop until next sound** option if you want the sound to be repeated until another sound is played.

If you wish to remove the sound transition effect applied to a slide, open the Sound list and choose the [No Sound] option. The [Stop Previous Sound] option stops a sound when the Loop until next sound option is active.

▪ To retest the chosen sound, click the ▶ Play button on the **Slide Transition** task pane or click the ⚝ symbol next to the slide thumbnail (if a visual transition has also been applied).

▪ If you previously selected the slides concerned, you do not need to confirm. If you made no selection and you want to apply your transition effect to all the slides in the presentation, click the **Apply to All Slides** button on the task pane.

Below you can see **Practice Exercise** 5.1. This exercise is made up of 8 steps. If you do not know how to do one of the steps, go back to the title that corresponds to that particular lesson. When you have finished, you can check your work by reading the **Solution** that follows.

Steps that are likely to be tested during the MOUS exam are marked with this symbol: ▦. However, it is a good idea to complete the whole exercise to ensure you have understood everything covered in the lesson.

☞ Practice Exercise 5.1

*To work on exercise 5.1, you should open the **5-1 Music.ppt** presentation, which is in the **MOUS PowerPoint 2002** folder.*

▦ 1. Set up the slide show so only the first three slides are played. Choose yellow as the pen colour.

▦ 2. Start the slide show and on the first slide, run the animation that is programmed on the guitar.

▦ 3. Scroll through the slide show until the end.

4. Start the slide show again and go to slide **2**. Use the pen to draw a circle around the text **Halford Community Centre**. Display the pointer as an arrow again.

5. On slide **2**, enter the following note: **Class times will be released on April 25**. Finish watching the slide show to the end.

▦ 6. Set **10** second timings for all the slides in the presentation. Run the slide show again, using all the slides.

▦ 7. To all the slides in the presentation, apply the transition effect called **Newsflash**, at **Medium** speed. To see the result of the effect, do not run the slide show, simply make a test.

⊞ 8. Associate the **Chime** sound with the transition effect on all the slides in the presentation. Run the slide show again, from beginning to end.
Finish by saving and closing the presentation.

If you want to put what you have learnt into practice on a real document, you can work on summary exercise 5 for the SLIDE SHOWS section, that you can find at the end of this book.

SLIDE SHOWS
Exercise 5.1: Working with slide shows

It is often possible to perform a task in several different ways, but here only the easiest solution is presented. You can go back to the corresponding lesson if you want to see other techniques you could use.

Solution to Exercise 5.1

1. To set up the slide show so only the first three slides are played, use the **Slide Show - Set Up Show** command. In the **Show slides** frame, type **1** in the **From** box and **3** in the **To** box (you can use the increment buttons if you wish).

    To change the pen colour, open the **Pen color** list and choose the colour yellow. Click **OK** to close the dialog box.

2. To start the slide show, press the F5 key. To run the animation that is programmed on the guitar, click the picture of the guitar on the first slide.

3. To scroll through the slide show until the end, click each slide as many times as necessary until you reach the end of the show.

4. To start the slide show again, press F5. Click twice to go to slide **2**. To use the pen to draw on the slide, press Ctrl **P** then drag to draw a circle around the **Halford Community Centre** text. To display the pointer as an arrow again, press Ctrl **A**.

5. To enter the note described in step 5 on slide 2, click the button in the bottom left corner of the slide then choose the **Speaker Notes** option. In the message box, type **Class times will be released on April 25** then click the **Close** button.

    To finish watching the slide show, click as many times as necessary.

6. To set 10 second timings for all the slides in the presentation, use **Slide Show - Slide Transition**. Under **Advance slide**, activate the **Automatically after** option and type **10** into the accompanying text box (or use the increment buttons). Click the **Apply to All Slides** button.

To run all the slides in the slide show, use the **Slide Show - Set Up Show** command. In the **Show slides** frame, tick the **All** option and in the **Advance slides** frame, tick the **Using timings, if present** option (if necessary). Click **OK** to confirm.

Use F5 to start the slide show and let it run to the end. When you reach the end, click to exit the slide show.

7. To apply the "Newsflash" effect at medium speed to all the slides in the presentation, scroll through the **Apply to selected slides** list in the **Slide Transition** task pane and click the **Newsflash** option. Open the **Speed** list and choose the **Medium** option then click the **Apply to All Slides** button.

To test the effect produced, click the ▶ Play button on the task pane.

8. To add the "Chime" sound to the transition effects on all the slides in the presentation, open the **Sound** list in the **Modify transition** section (if PowerPoint asks you to install a component, click **Yes** and follow the instructions) and choose the **Chime** sound. Click the **Apply to All Slides** button.

To run the slide show, press F5. Let the show run and when you reach the end, click to exit the slide show.

To save and close the presentation, use **File - Close** and click **Yes** when PowerPoint asks you if you want to save the presentation.

SLIDE SHOWS
Exercise 5.1: Working with slide shows

SLIDE SHOWS
Lesson 5.2: Animations

1 ▪ Previewing an animation effect

*An **animation** is a special sound or visual effect that you can apply to text or objects and which appears during the slide show. You can preview an animation's effects before running your slide show.*

▪ If necessary, display the **Custom Animation** task pane with the **Slide Show - Custom Animation** command.

▪ Access the slide whose animation effects you want to view.

▪ Click the ▶ Play button on the task pane.

Start:	🖱 On Click	▼
Direction:		**Speed:**
In	▼	Very Fast ▼

Do Re Mi

;sons for children and adults
welcome

```
1 ⚡ j0225180
2 ⚡ j0225180
3 ⚡ j0129643
4 ⚡ j0129643
5 ⚡ j0129643
6 ⚡ j0232478
7 ⚡ j0232478
```

Seconds ▼ ◄ 0 | 2 ► ►

🔼 Re-Order 🔽

■ Stop   📽 Slide Show

☑ AutoPreview

*You will view all the slide's animations, except for any that must be started by clicking another object. The **Play** button becomes a* ■ Stop *button, which you can click to stop the animation preview.*
A timeline appears in the task pane at the bottom of the animation list and shows the timing of each animation effect in seconds.

To start the slide show from the active slide and view all the animation effects, click the 📽 Slide Show button on the task pane.

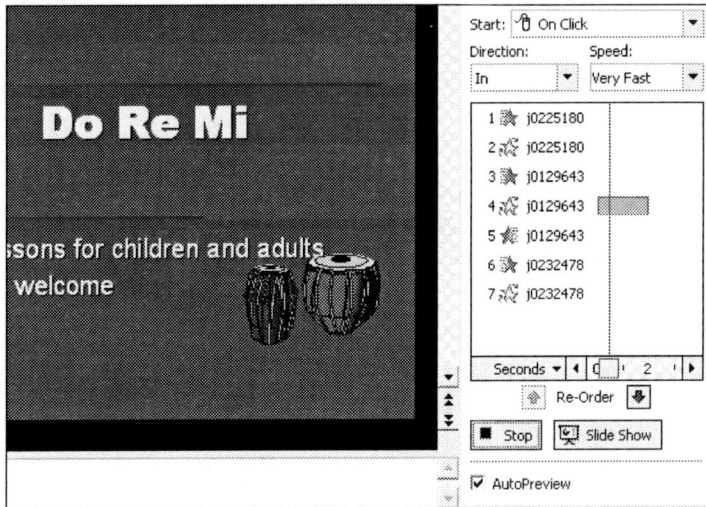

2 ▪ Applying an animation scheme

An animation scheme is a collection of predefined animation effects that you can apply to text placeholders. These animations appear during the slide show.

▪ Select the slides to which you wish to apply an animation effect.

▪ Display the **Slide Design - Animation Schemes** task pane or use the **Slide Show - Animation Schemes** command.

▪ Choose an animation scheme from the **Apply to selected slides** list.

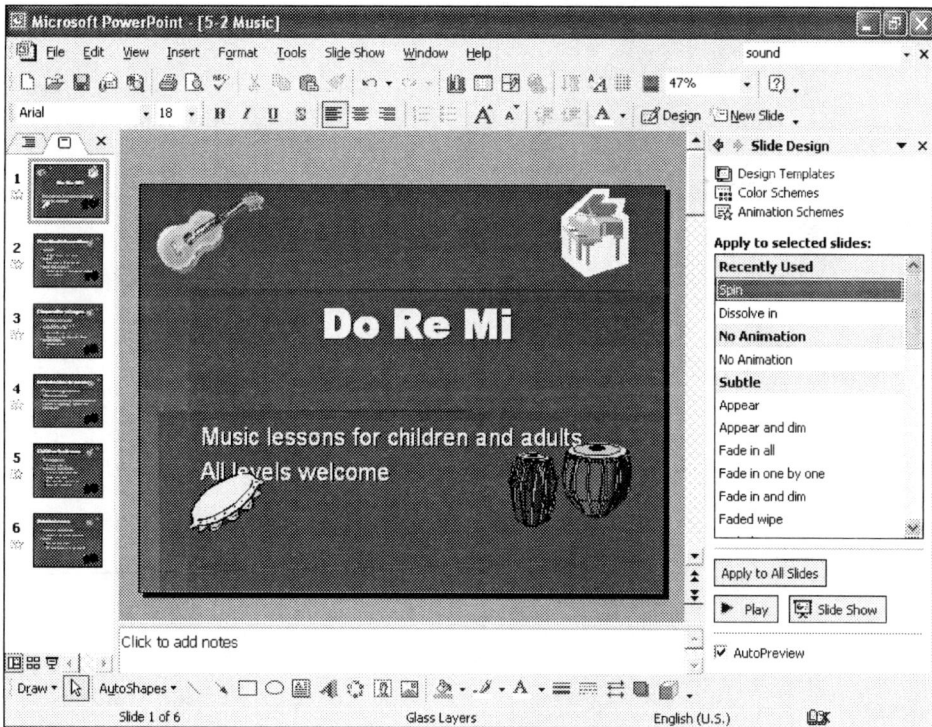

*If the **AutoPreview** check box is active at the bottom of the task pane, PowerPoint will demonstrate the effect produced. When a slide is associated with an animation scheme, the ⚏ symbol appears next to, or underneath, the slide thumbnail (this depends on the active view).*

- If you previously selected the slides concerned, you need take no further action. If you did not select any slides and you want to apply your animation scheme to all the slides in the presentation, click the **Apply to All Slides** option.

- To retest an animation scheme, click the ▶ Play button in the task pane.

Applying an animation scheme to all the slides is equivalent to applying an animation effect to the placeholders in the slide master.

*To cancel an animation scheme, choose the **No Animation** option in the **Apply to selected slides** list of the **Slide Design - Animation Schemes** task pane.*

3 ▪ Applying an animation to an object

PowerPoint provides many animation effects that you can apply to objects or placeholders on a slide. These animation effects run during the slide show.

- Select the object concerned. If you want your animation scheme to act simultaneously with several objects, select the object(s) concerned.

  You can select all or part of a text placeholder. You can also work in Slide Master view.

- Display the **Custom Animation** task pane or use the **Slide Show - Custom Animation** command.

- Click the [⭐ Add Effect ▼] button and choose one of the following effects from the list:

Entrance the object will perform an animation effect when it appears on the slide.

Emphasis the object will be animated after it has appeared on the slide.

Exit the object will disappear with an animation effect.

Motion Paths the object will move in a specific direction (for example, rotate) after it has appeared on the slide.

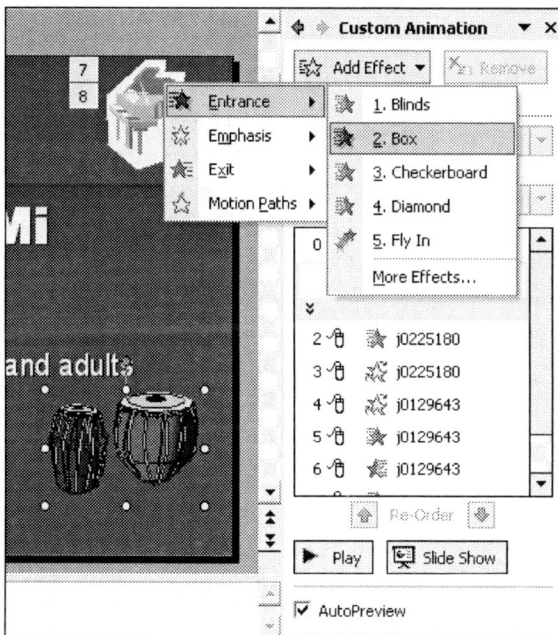

*You can use the **More Effects** and **More Motion Paths** options to choose other effects that are not in the list.*

- Choose the required effect.

  If the **AutoPreview** check box is active at the bottom of the task pane, PowerPoint will demonstrate the chosen animation.

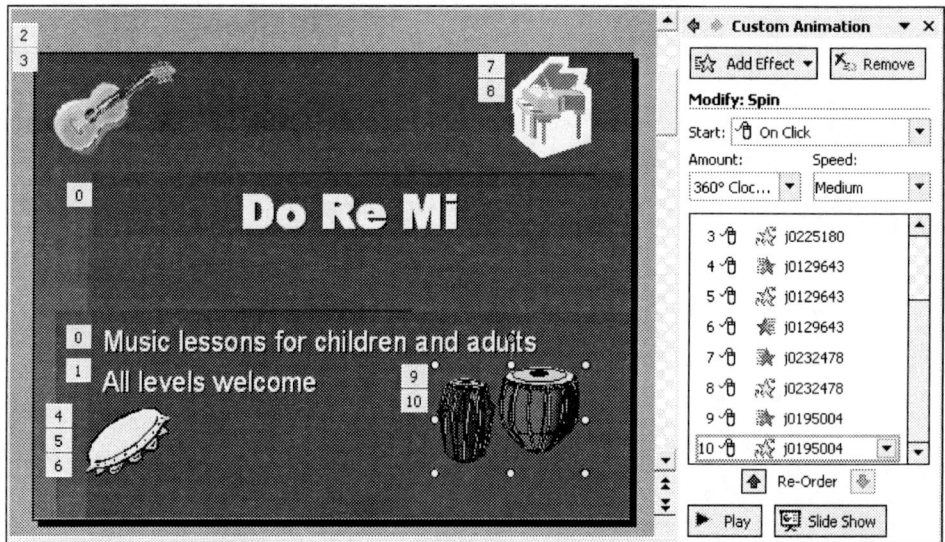

The animation effect appears in the list on the **Custom Animation** task pane. It carries the name of the object to which you applied it. To the left of this name, you can see a number showing where it is in the order of animations, a symbol to indicate how it starts and a symbol to indicate the type of effect.

Non-printing numbered tags appear in the slide, to link the animated objects with the effects in the list. These tags appear only in Normal view when the **Custom Animation** task pane is on screen.

⁑ You can customise the settings of an effect using the options in the second list in the **Modify** frame.

The name of this list depends on the effect you select; it may be called **Property**, **Direction**, **Size**, **Amount** or **Path**.

When an object has an animation effect, the ⁂ icon appears next to or underneath the thumbnail of the slide containing it.

When you create an animation effect for a placeholder that contains several paragraph levels, the effect will run simultaneously on each main paragraph and any sub-paragraphs associated with it. The **Custom Animation** task pane presents a collapsed list containing an animation effect for each main paragraph and the sub-paragraphs created from it. To expand the list, click the [≫] arrow. To collapse the list again, click the [≪] arrow (which appears after the last effect).

Here, an animation scheme has been applied to this placeholder, which contains 5 paragraphs:

1	▸ Distance running
1	– From 10km to marathon training
1	– Group runs, endurance training
1	▸ Nutritional advice also available
2	▸ Training sessions from Nov-May (weather conditions allowing)

Collapsed list: 1 ⌄Ö ⭑ Text 2: Distance r...
                 ≫

Expanded list: 1 ⌄Ö ⭑ Distance running
                      ⭑ From 10km to mar...
                      ⭑ Group runs, endur...
                      ⭑ Nutritional advice ...
                2 ⌄Ö ⭑ Training sessions f...
                ≪

Whether they are customised or not, **Motion Paths** effects appear in slides as dotted lines (in Normal view, with the **Custom Animation** task pane open). A green arrow marks the path's starting point and a red arrow marks its end point and the direction in which it will travel.

📄 *For sound objects, in addition to **Entrance, Emphasis, Exit** and **Motion Paths** effects, you can add **Sound Actions: Play, Pause** or **Stop**.*

🔍 *You can apply several different effects to the same object, for example, an entrance effect, an emphasis effect, a motion path and an exit effect, or you could apply several entrance effects to make the object appear several times (with a different effect each time).*

4 ▪ **Managing animation effects**

Selecting an animation effect

▪ If necessary, display the **Custom Animation** task pane or use the **Slide Show - Custom Animation** command.

▪ To select all the effects associated with a given object, select that object.

▪ Click the required animation effect in the task pane.
or
Click its numbered tag in the slide.

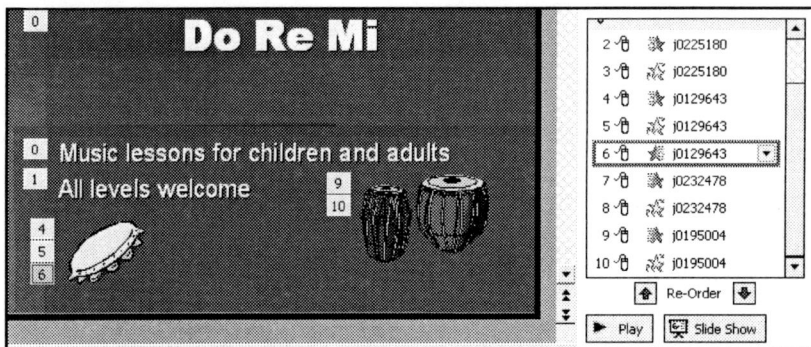

A coloured border appears around the animation effect and an arrow appears to the right: click this arrow to open the animation effect's drop-down list.

When you point to an effect in the task pane list, a ScreenTip indicates how the animation effect starts, its name and the name of the animated object.

Replacing an animation effect by another

» If necessary, display the **Custom Animation** task pane or use the **Slide Show - Custom Animation** command.

» Select the animation effect you want to change.

» Click the ☆ Change ▼ button and choose a different effect.

Removing an animation effect

» If necessary, display the **Custom Animation** task pane.

» To remove all the effects associated with an object, select the object.

To remove an individual animation effect, select the effect and not the object.

» Click the ✕ Remove button or open the effect's drop-down list in the task pane and choose the **Remove** option.

When you remove an animation effect, PowerPoint automatically renumbers the other animations on the slide.

Changing the order of animation effects

» In the task pane, select the required animation effect or the group of effects applied to the same object.

When a slide has several animation effects, by default, they appear from top to bottom in the list in the order you created them.

» Drag the animation upwards or downwards in the list.

A thick black horizontal line indicates the new position in the list.

* When you reach the required position, release the mouse button.

  PowerPoint renumbers the effects accordingly.

You can also use the ⬆ *and/or* ⬇ *button to move the effect(s) upwards and/or downwards in the list.*

⊞5 • Inserting a hyperlink

A hyperlink is an object or text which you can click in order to go directly to an existing file or Web page, a specific place in a document or a new mail message using an e-mail address.
A hyperlink can be activated while you are viewing the slide show in PowerPoint or when the presentation is shown in a browser.

* Place the insertion point in the text box in which the link reference is to be inserted, or select the text or object that is to be the link.

* **Insert - Hyperlink** or 🖱 or Ctrl **K**

* Click the **ScreenTip** button if you want to give a descriptive text that will appear in a ScreenTip when you point to the hyperlink.

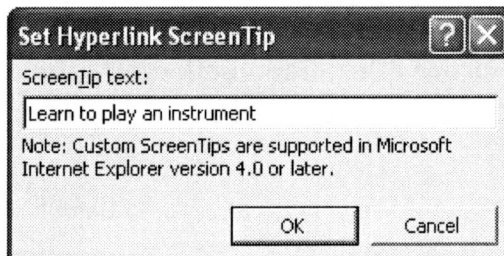

Set Hyperlink ScreenTip	? X
ScreenTip text:	
Learn to play an instrument	
Note: Custom ScreenTips are supported in Microsoft Internet Explorer version 4.0 or later.	
OK	Cancel

* Click **OK**.

■ Choose the sort of hyperlink you want to create by clicking one of the shortcuts on the **Link to** Places Bar:

Existing File or Web Page	To fill in the **Address** box, you should type the name of the document referred to by the link or select one of the available links (click the **Current Folder** shortcut and use the **Look in** list to choose a file on your computer or network, click the **Recent Files** button to see a list of recently used files or click the **Browsed Pages** button to see addresses of Web pages that you have already visited). If you wish, use the **Bookmark** button to go to a named location in a document to which you can create the hyperlink.
Place in This Document	Select the slide that should be activated when you click the hyperlink. To select a slide by its title click the + sign that precedes the **Slide Titles** option and click the slide you want.

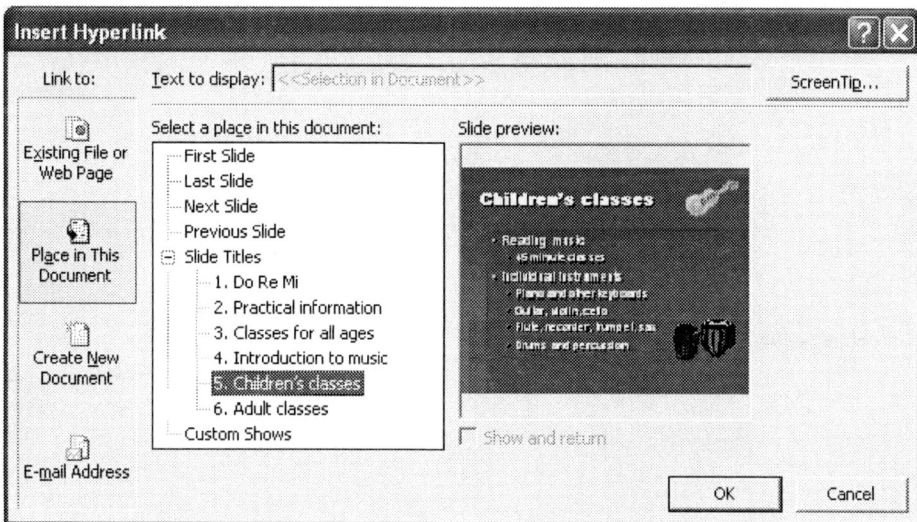

Create New Document	Give the **Name of new document** and choose whether you want to **Edit the new document later** or **now** (whichever option you choose, PowerPoint creates the presentation, but it does not contain any slides: you will have to create them).
E-mail Address	A new mail message will be created when you click the link; indicate the **E-mail address** and the message **Subject** which will appear systematically in the message window.

* Click **OK**.

In Normal, Slide Sorter or Notes Page view the hyperlink text is shown in blue and underlined. Hyperlinks on objects do not appear.

When you run the slide show or if you preview the presentation in a browser the mouse pointer takes the shape of a hand when you point (without clicking) to the link. The text you gave as a ScreenTip (if you did) also appears.

Below you can see **Practice Exercise** 5.2. This exercise is made up of 5 steps. If you do not know how to do one of the steps, go back to the title that corresponds to that particular lesson. When you have finished, you can check your work by reading the **Solution** that follows.

Steps that are likely to be tested during the MOUS exam are marked with this symbol: 🔲. However, it is a good idea to complete the whole exercise to ensure you have understood everything covered in the lesson.

☞ Practice Exercise 5.2

To work on exercise 5.2, you should open the **5-2 Music.ppt** presentation, which is in the **MOUS PowerPoint 2002** folder.

1. This presentation already contains animation effects. Preview the animations on the first slide.

🔲 2. Apply a **Spin** animation scheme to all the slides in the presentation.

3. On the first slide, apply these animation effects to the picture of the drums: a **Box** entrance effect and a **Spin** emphasis effect.

4. Select the **Checkerboard** exit effect on the tambourine then remove this effect.

🔲 5. Insert a hyperlink on the piano object that will take you to the fifth slide in the presentation, called **Children's classes**. When you point to the object, the text **Learn to play an instrument** should appear in a ScreenTip.
Finish by saving and closing the presentation.

If you want to put what you have learnt into practice on a real document, you can work on summary exercise 5 for the SLIDE SHOWS section, that you can find at the end of this book.

It is often possible to perform a task in several different ways, but here only the easiest solution is presented. You can go back to the corresponding lesson if you want to see other techniques you could use.

Solution to Exercise 5.2

1. To preview the animation effects applied to the first slide, use **Slide Show - Custom Animation** and in the task pane, click the ▶ Play button.

2. To apply a "Spin" animation scheme to all the slides in the presentation, use **Slide Show - Animation Schemes**. On the task pane, go to the **Apply to selected slides** list, click the **Spin** animation scheme (in the **Moderate** effects) and click the **Apply to All Slides** button.

3. To apply the specified animation effects on the drums on the first slide, click the picture of the drums to select it.

    Use **Slide Show - Custom Animation** then click the ⬚ Add Effect ▼ button and point to the **Entrance** option. From the list that opens, choose the **Box** option.

    Keep the object selected, click the ⬚ Add Effect ▼ button again, choose the **Emphasis** option and, in the list, choose the **Spin** option.

4. To select the "Checkerboard" effect that is on the tambourine, click the tambourine then, in the task pane list, look at the three effects applied to this object. Click the effect that is symbolised by a red star (if you point to it, you will see **Checkerboard** in the ScreenTip).

    To remove this effect, click the ✖ Remove button in the task pane.

5. To insert a hyperlink on the piano object that will take you to the fifth slide in the presentation, click the piano object to select it.

Use the **Insert - Hyperlink** command.

To make the text "Learn to play an instrument" appear in a ScreenTip when you point to the piano, click the **ScreenTip** button and in the text box, enter **Learn to play an instrument** then click **OK**.

On the **Link to** Places Bar, click **Place in This Document** then if necessary, click the + sign that precedes **Slide Titles** in the **Select a place in this document** list and click slide **5. Children's classes**.

Click **OK** to confirm and close the **Insert Hyperlink** dialog box.

To save and close the presentation, use **File - Close** and click **Yes** when PowerPoint asks if you want to save the presentation.

EXCHANGING DATA
Lesson 6.1: Working with other applications

1 ▪ **Copying data from Microsoft Word or Excel**

You can make a simple copy of data in Word or Excel and paste it into a PowerPoint slide without creating a link. Any changes that you make to this data in PowerPoint will not affect the source documents; any changes made to the original document will not be carried over into the PowerPoint presentation.

❋ Start the Microsoft Word or Microsoft Excel application and open the document containing the data you wish to copy. Select this data (it may be text, a table, a chart and so on).

❋ **Edit - Copy** or ▣ or ⌨ Ctrl **C**

❋ Go to the target presentation in PowerPoint and activate the slide in which the copied data should appear.

❋ **Edit - Paste Special**

*You could also use the **Paste** option in the **Edit** menu to paste in data from another application, but you cannot choose the format in this case.*

❋ In the **Paste Special** dialog box, make sure the **Paste** option is active.

❋ In the **As** list, choose the format in which the data should be pasted into the PowerPoint presentation.

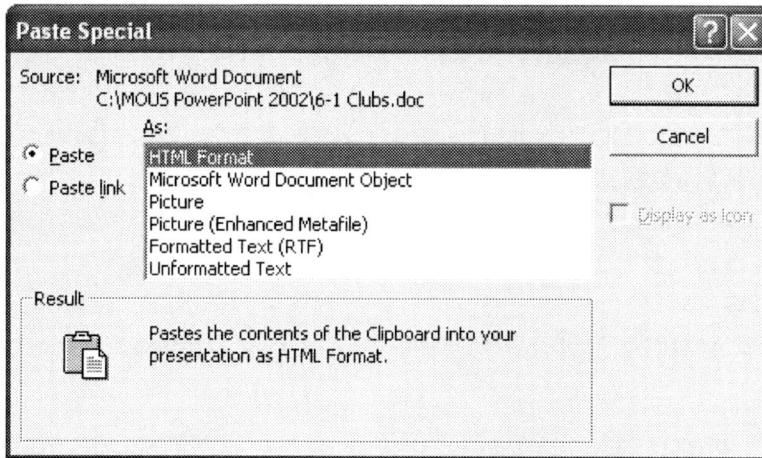

The **HTML Format** option produces the same effect as using the **Edit - Paste** command. The **[name of application] Object** option (for example **Microsoft Excel Worksheet Object, Microsoft Word Document Object** or **Microsoft Excel Chart Object**) pastes the object and will open the source application any time you edit the pasted data. If you choose this format, the **Display as icon** option becomes available and you can choose to display the data as an icon.

* Click **OK**.

When you paste in a picture, a diagram, a chart or a table, the [⚡] button may appear. To integrate the new object, PowerPoint adjusts the slide layout automatically. You can cancel the layout PowerPoint applied or even deactivate that feature altogether: click the [⚡] button and choose to **Undo Automatic Layout** or **Stop Automatic Layout of Inserted Objects**.

📖2 ▪ Copying data from Word or Excel with a link

If you create a link when you copy data from Word or Excel, any changes made to the pasted data are carried over into the original source document. In the same way, changes made to the original document will also occur in the pasted data in PowerPoint.

⁕ Start the Microsoft Word or Excel application then open the document containing the data you wish to copy and link. Select the data concerned (text, a table, a chart etc.).

⁕ **Edit - Copy** or [📋] or [Ctrl] **C**

⁕ Go to the target presentation in PowerPoint and activate the slide in which the pasted data should appear.

⁕ **Edit - Paste Special**

⁕ Activate the **Paste link** option.

⁕ In the **As** list, choose how the data should appear in the PowerPoint presentation.

The option names differ according to the type of object being pasted.

⁕ Activate the **Display as icon** option to show the pasted data only as an icon.

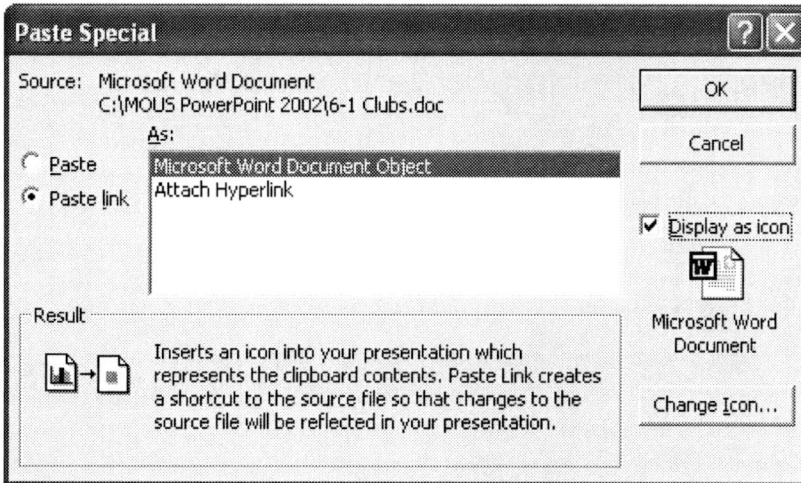

When the **Display as icon** option is active, you can click the **Change Icon** button to change the icon's appearance.

If you display the pasted data as an icon, you can see the data from the presentation by double-clicking the icon.

▪ Click **OK**.

If both applications are open, any changes made to the source or client document will be carried over immediately into the other. Otherwise, when you open the presentation (or Word or Excel), a message will appear to prompt you to update the changes.

If the object was pasted as an icon, double-click the icon to edit the object. If you want it to open during the slide show, select the pasted item then use **Slide Show - Action Settings**. Choose a tab, depending on which event should trigger the object, activate the **Object action** option and choose whether the object should **Open** or whether you wish to **Edit** it.

▥3 ▪ Creating a new object from another application

▪ In PowerPoint, activate the slide in which you wish to create the new object.

▪ **Insert - Object**

▪ Make sure the **Create new** option is active.

▪ In the **Object type** list, click the sort of object you wish to create.

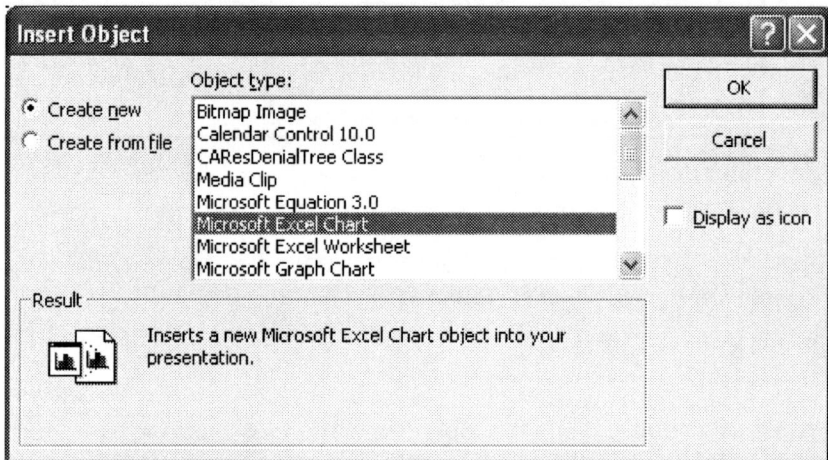

▪ Activate the **Display as icon** option if you want the new object to appear as an icon only.

▪ Click **OK**.

*If the **Display as icon** option is active, the other application will open in a separate window. Otherwise, the application opens within PowerPoint.*

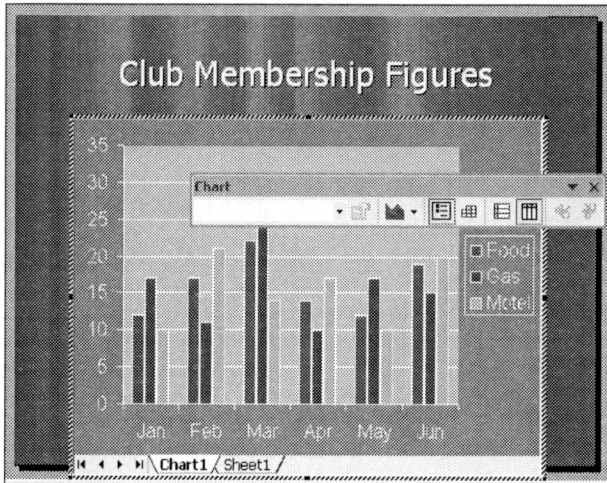

*In this example, the object created is a **Microsoft Excel Chart**; the **Chart1** sheet is active and shows a chart made with sample data.*

* Finish making the object.

  *If you wish to finish making an **Microsoft Excel Chart** with your own data, click the **Sheet1** sheet tab, delete the sample data shown and enter your own table of data.*

* If the object is being created in the source application window, use the **Close & Return to [name of presentation]** command. If you are creating it with the other application's tools and menus within PowerPoint, click outside the object to return to PowerPoint.

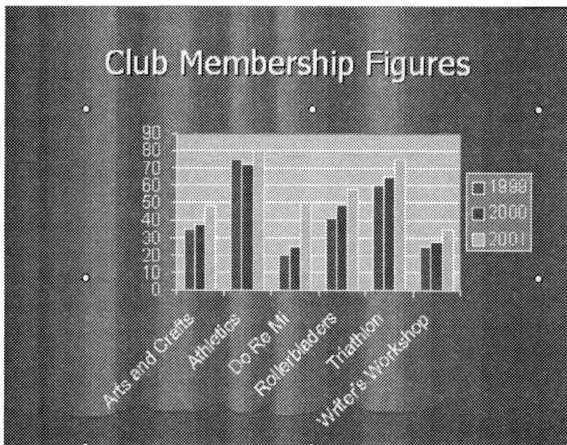

If you are embedding an Excel object, remember to activate the correct worksheet or chart sheet before you return to PowerPoint.

📄 *To modify an object created in this way, double-click the object.*

📖 4 ▪ **Inserting a file as an object**

You can insert a document from another application, so it will appear in your presentation as an object.

▪ In PowerPoint, go into the presentation concerned and activate the slide in which you want the object to appear.

▪ **Insert - Object**

▪ Activate the **Create from file** option.

▪ Click the **Browse** button and choose the document you want to insert.

▪ If you want any future changes made to the object to be taken into account in the presentation, activate the **Link** option.

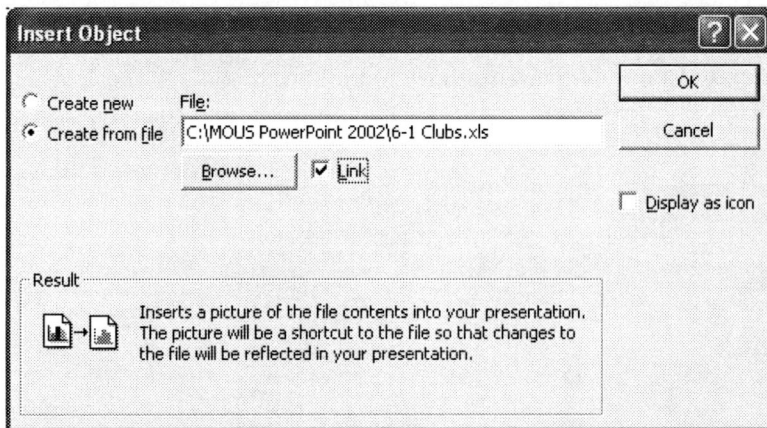

Insert Object   ❓ ✖

                File: **OK**

○ Create new

● Create from file   `C:\MOUS PowerPoint 2002\6-1 Clubs.xls`   **Cancel**

             Browse...   ☑ Link

                                    ☐ Display as icon

Result

   Inserts a picture of the file contents into your presentation. The picture will be a shortcut to the file so that changes to the file will be reflected in your presentation.

If you do not activate this option, PowerPoint will embed the object rather than linking to it.

▪ If you want PowerPoint to display the object as an icon rather than displaying the object's contents, activate the **Display as icon** option.

▪ Click **OK**.

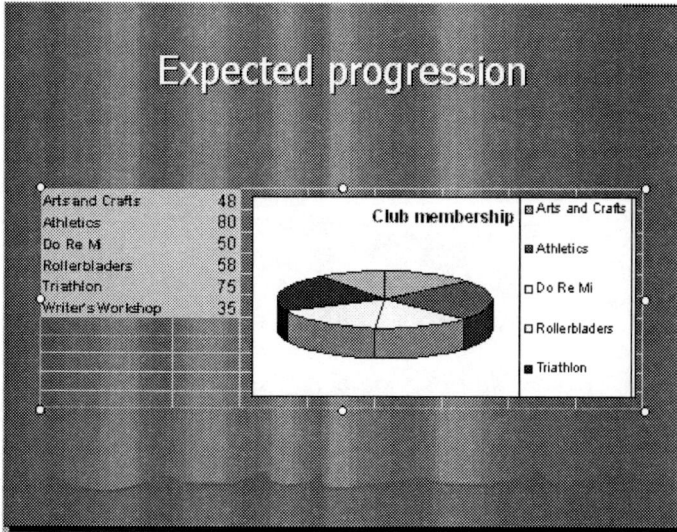

No matter what type of object it is, you can move or animate this object, as you would any other.

If you did not activate the **Display as icon** option, the inserted object appears as it would in its source application; otherwise, an icon appears to symbolise the object.

* To open an inserted object, double-click it.

If you inserted the object as an icon, the source application starts and the document appears. You can modify this document then return to PowerPoint using the **Close & Return to [name of presentation]** command. If you embedded the object (and did not link it), double-click it to open it in a hatched border; the source application's menus and tools replace those of PowerPoint. To return to PowerPoint, click outside the object.

* If you want to be able to open an object that is displayed as an icon during a slide show, select the object then use **Slide Show - Action Settings**. Choose a tab, depending on which event should trigger the object, activate the **Object action** option and choose whether the object should **Open** or whether you wish to **Edit** it.

Using this same technique, you can also insert one presentation within another.

Below you can see **Practice Exercise** 6.1. This exercise is made up of 4 steps. If you do not know how to do one of the steps, go back to the title that corresponds to that particular lesson. When you have finished, you can check your work by reading the **Solution** that follows.

All the steps in this exercise are likely to be tested in the MOUS exam.

☞ Practice Exercise 6.1

*To work on exercise 6.1, you should open the **6-1 Clubs.ppt** presentation, which is in the **MOUS PowerPoint 2002** folder.*

1. On the third slide of the presentation, import the first table from the Word document called **6-1 Clubs.doc** (this is in the **MOUS PowerPoint 2002** folder). Paste the data in HTML format and cancel the automatic layout.

2. On the fifth slide of the presentation, link the data from the second table in the Word document called **6-1 Clubs.doc** (in the **MOUS PowerPoint 2002** folder). Insert this data in the form of an icon.

3. On the fourth slide in the presentation, insert an Excel chart object and in it, show the following data (you should enter this data in the **Sheet1** worksheet):

	A	B	C	D
1		1999	2000	2001
2	Arts and Crafts	35	38	48
3	Athletics	75	72	80
4	Do Re Mi	20	25	50
5	Rollerbladers	41	49	58
6	Triathlon	60	65	75
7	Writer's Workshop	25	28	35

4. On the last slide in the presentation, insert the Excel file called **6-1 Clubs.xls**, which is in the **MOUS PowerPoint 2002** folder. Insert it as a linked object.
Finish by saving and closing the **6-1 Clubs** presentation.

If you want to put what you have learnt into practice on a real document, you can work on summary exercise 6 for the EXCHANGING DATA section, that you can find at the end of this book.

It is often possible to perform a task in several different ways, but here only the easiest solution is presented. You can go back to the corresponding lesson if you want to see other techniques you could use.

Solution to Exercise 6.1

1. To insert the first table from the 6-1 Clubs.doc document into the third slide of the presentation, start by opening the **Microsoft Word** application (use the **Start** menu on the Windows taskbar, for example). Use the **File - Open** command, browse to find the **MOUS PowerPoint 2002** folder then double-click to open the **6-1 Clubs.doc** document. Click inside the first table and use **Table - Select - Table**. Use **Edit - Copy** to transfer the table into the clipboard.

   On the taskbar, click the button for the **6-1 Clubs.ppt** PowerPoint presentation then activate the third slide in the presentation by clicking its thumbnail in the **Slides** tab.

   Use the **Edit - Paste Special** command. Keep the **Paste** option active and choose **HTML Format** in the **As** list (if necessary). Click **OK**.

   To cancel the automatic layout, click the 🔣 button that appears and choose the **Undo Automatic Layout** option.

2. To link the data from the second table in the 6-1 Clubs.doc document into the fifth slide in the presentation, return to the **6-1 Clubs.doc** document in Word by clicking its button on the taskbar.

   Select the second table by dragging over it. Use **Edit - Copy** to copy the data into the clipboard.

   On the taskbar, click the button that corresponds to the **6-1 Clubs.ppt** presentation to return to PowerPoint then activate the fifth slide in the presentation by clicking its thumbnail in the **Slides** tab.

   Use the **Edit - Paste Special** command.

Activate the **Paste link** option then tick the **Display as icon** check box.

Click **OK**.

3. To insert an Excel chart object on the fourth slide in the presentation, click the thumbnail of the fourth slide to activate it.

Use **Insert - Object**, make sure the **Create new** option is active and in the **Object type** list, choose the **Microsoft Excel Chart** option. Click **OK**.

When the Excel application starts, click **Sheet1** on the object then enter the data as shown in step 3. You can use **View - Zoom** to adjust the zoom if necessary.

Enter the data in the first column (you may have to adjust its width by double-clicking the vertical line to the right of the column). Once you have entered the data, choose a **Fit** zoom type.
Click the **Chart1** tab then click outside the Excel object.

4. To insert the Excel file called 6-1 Clubs.xls as a linked object in the last slide in the presentation, click the thumbnail of the last slide in the **Slides** tab to activate it.

Use **Insert - Object**; activate the **Create from file** option then click the **Browse** button. Go to the **MOUS PowerPoint 2002** folder and choose the **6-1 Clubs.xls** workbook then click **OK**.

In the **Insert Object** dialog box, tick the **Link** check box then click **OK**.

To save and close the presentation, use the **File - Close** command and click **Yes** when PowerPoint asks if you wish to save before closing.

EXCHANGING DATA
Lesson 6.2: Group work

1 ▪ Managing comments

This technique enables you to add a comment to a slide in a presentation that you are sending for review.

Creating a comment

▪ Go to the slide in which you wish to add a comment and, if necessary, select the object to which the comment will refer.

▪ **Insert - Comment** or

*This tool button can be found on the **Reviewing** toolbar.*

A comment box appears in the top left corner of the slide, containing the user's name and the day's date. A tag, giving the user's initials and the comment number, is associated with the comment box.

▪ Enter your required text then click outside the comment box.

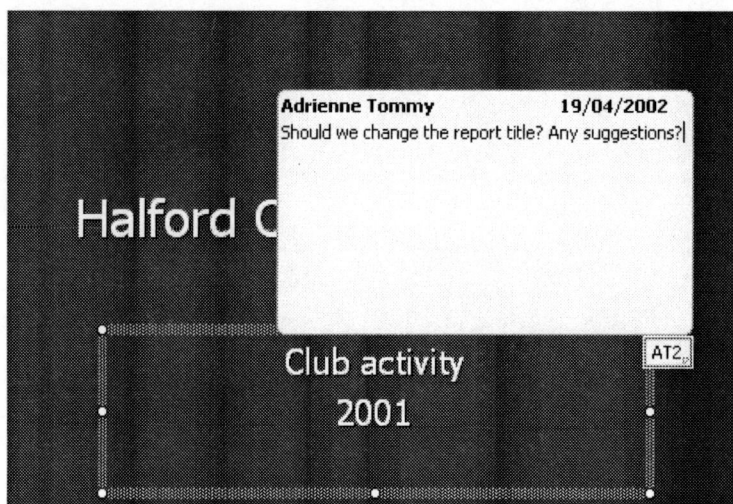

Adrienne Tommy   19/04/2002
Should we change the report title? Any suggestions?

Halford C

Club activity
2001

AT2

To see a preview of the comment's contents, simply point to the associated tag.

Modifying a comment

※ If they are hidden, display the comment tags with the **View - Markup** command or 🖉 on the **Reviewing** toolbar.

※ Double-click the tag of the comment you wish to edit.

※ Make your changes then click outside the comment box to confirm.

Moving/deleting a comment

※ To move a comment, select its tag then drag it to the required position.

※ To delete a comment, select it then press the Del key.

Moving from one comment to another

※ If it is not on display, show the **Reviewing** toolbar with **View - Toolbars - Reviewing**.

※ Click ⬅ to go to the previous comment or ➡ to go to the next one.

2 ▪ Sending a presentation for review

You can send a presentation by Outlook to other users who can add their own comments to it or edit their own copies of the presentation. This avoids having to refer to a printed copy of the document. Both you and the message recipients must be using Microsoft Outlook as your e-mail application.

※ Open the presentation you wish to send for review.

※ **File - Send To - Mail Recipient (for Review)**

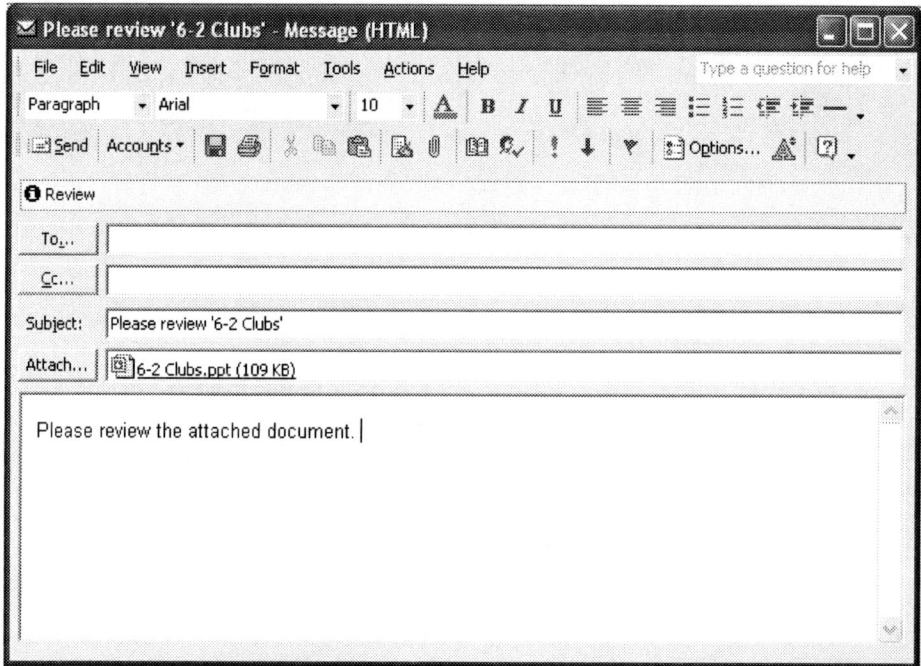

A new e-mail message window opens, with your presentation added as an attachment. The message's subject and the main message text remind the addressee that you want him/her to review the document.

» Give the e-mail address(es) of the message recipient(s) in the **To** and/or **Cc** boxes.

» If you wish, complete or edit the message **Subject** and the main message text.

» Click the ⌨ **Send** button on the message window.

*Each addressee receives the message, accompanied by a review flag ▼. To modify the presentation, he/she must double-click the attached file's name in Outlook. Once the required changes have been made, the presentation can be sent back to you with **File - Send To - Original Sender**.*

📄 *Only the author of the presentation that was sent for review will see the changes that the reviewers have made to the presentation. When the reviewer saves the revised copy of the presentation, this does not affect the author's original presentation.*

▦3 ▪ Managing reviewers' changes

Merging reviewed presentations

Once your reviewers have returned their revised presentations to you, via Outlook, you can merge their changes with your original presentation, so that you can see all the comments and changes in a single document.

▪ In Outlook, double-click the attachment corresponding to the presentation you want to merge.

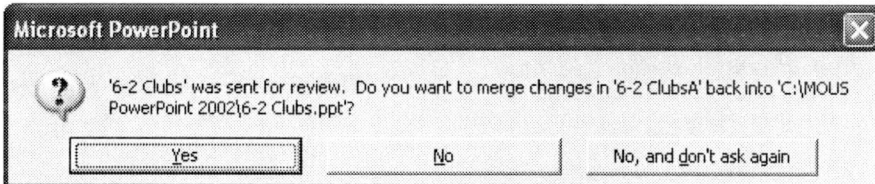

A message appears, offering to merge the attached file.

▪ Click **Yes** to accept the merge.

EXCHANGING DATA
Lesson 6.2: Group work

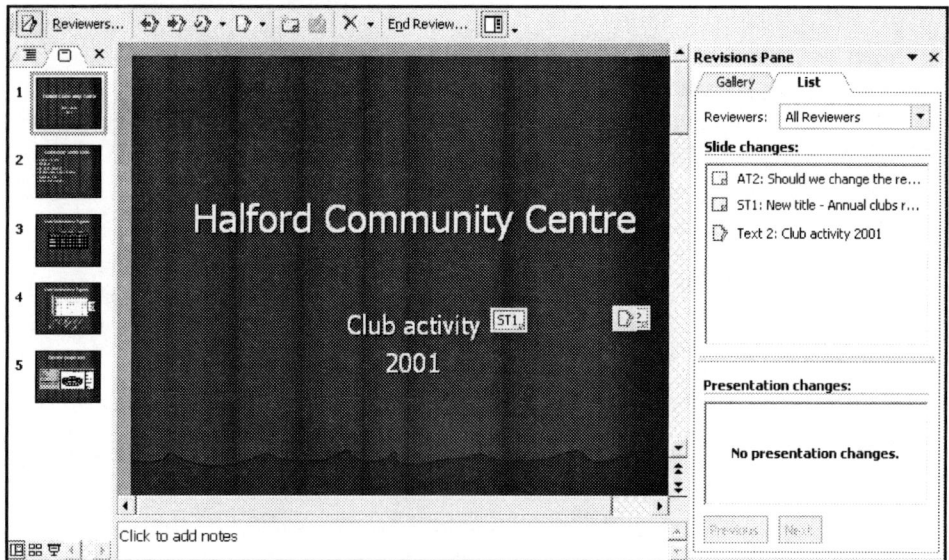

PowerPoint 2002 automatically merges the reviewed presentation file with your original presentation. The **Revisions Pane** appears. This pane contains two tabs: the **Gallery** tab and the **List** tab.

Comment colours and change markers identify each reviewer's comments and modifications. PowerPoint also identifies any conflicting changes from the reviewers.

To merge the presentations sent for review via a server or a hard disk, open the original presentation in PowerPoint 2002 and use the **Tools - Compare and Merge Presentations** command. Select the reviewed presentations you want to merge and click the **Merge** button.

Accepting reviewers' changes

» Use the [button] or [button] tool button to go to the previous or next comment.

All the changes appear in a box; each one is preceded by a check box.

Click the check box of each change that you wish to accept.

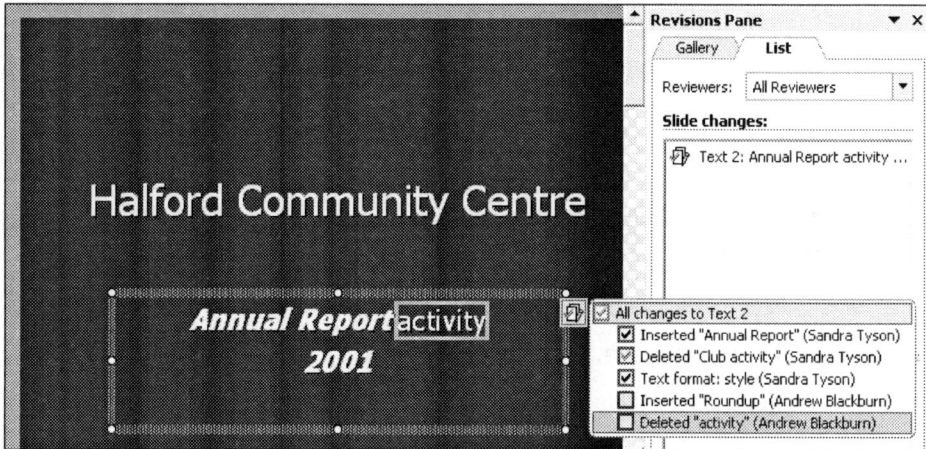

*You can also accept changes by clicking a change marker in the **List** tab then ticking the check box of each change you wish to keep in the presentation.*

To accept all the changes made on a particular slide or over the whole presentation, open the list on the [tool icon] tool button on the **Reviewing** toolbar then choose the **Apply All Changes to the Current Slide** or **Apply All Changes to the Presentation** option, depending on what you wish to accept.

To accept all the changes made by a particular reviewer on a particular slide, click the **Gallery** tab and point to the preview slide that contains changes by the reviewer whose changes you want to apply. Click the arrow that appears on the right of the slide and in the shortcut menu, click the **Apply Changes By This Reviewer** option.

To apply changes to the slide master, use **View - Master - Slide Master** then choose the modifications you wish to apply.

Reviewers' changes made to the Notes Page master or the Handout master are not taken into account when you merge reviewed presentations with your original.

Cancelling reviewers' changes

* To cancel a change you have applied, click its change marker then deactivate that change's check box or click the ![tool button] tool button on the **Reviewing** toolbar.

* To cancel all the changes, open the list on the ![tool button] tool button then choose the **Unapply all Changes to the Current Slide** or **Unapply All Changes to the Presentation** option, according to your needs.

Viewing a specific reviewer's changes

* Click the **Reviewers** button on the **Reviewing** toolbar or click the **List** tab on the **Revisions Pane** then select only the check box corresponding to the reviewer whose changes you want to see. You can also click the **Gallery** tab in the **Revisions Pane** and point to the slide that shows the changes from the reviewer concerned. Open the list by clicking the arrow that appears on the right side of the slide and choose the **Show Only This Reviewer's Changes** option.

Deleting all the changes made by a reviewer

* Click the **Gallery** tab in the **Revisions Pane** and point to the slide that shows the changes from the reviewer whose revisions you wish to delete. Open the list by clicking the arrow that appears on the right side of the slide and choose the **Done With This Reviewer** option.

> A reviewer should only be removed from a reviewed presentation once you are sure that you have applied all the required changes that he/she has suggested. Once you remove that reviewer's changes, all the information he/she suggested is deleted permanently.

Below you can see **Practice Exercise** 6.2. This exercise is made up of 3 steps. If you do not know how to do one of the steps, go back to the title that corresponds to that particular lesson. When you have finished, you can check your work by reading the **Solution** that follows.

All the steps in this exercise are likely to be tested in the MOUS exam.

☞ Practice Exercise 6.2

*To work on exercise 6.2, you should open the **6-2 Clubs.ppt** presentation, which is in the **MOUS PowerPoint 2002** folder.*

1. On the first slide, select the subtitle placeholder and create the following comment: **Should we change the report title? Any suggestions?**.

2. Send the **6-2 Clubs.ppt** presentation for review to any recipient(s) you like.

3. Open the **6-2 Clubs reviewed.ppt** presentation (this is in the MOUS PowerPoint 2002 folder). This is a simulation, as if you sent the 6-2 Clubs presentation to two reviewers (Sandra Tyson and Andrew Blackburn) who have reviewed it and returned it to you.

   Accept all the changes made by **Sandra Tyson** to the subtitle on the first slide.

   Save the **6-2 Clubs presentation** and close it.

If you want to put what you have learnt into practice on a real document, you can work on summary exercise 6 for the EXCHANGING DATA section, that you can find at the end of this book.

It is often possible to perform a task in several different ways, but here only the easiest solution is presented. You can go back to the corresponding lesson if you want to see other techniques you could use.

Solution to Exercise 6.2

1. To create the comment described in step 1, select the subtitle placeholder on slide 1. If the **Reviewing** toolbar is not on the screen, display it with **View - Toolbars - Reviewing**. Click the tool button and, in the comment box, type **Should we change the report title? Any suggestions?**.

2. To send the 6-2 Clubs.ppt presentation for review, to your choice of recipient(s), use the **File - Send To - Mail Recipient (for Review)** command. In the **To** and/or **Cc** text boxes, type the address(es) of the recipient(s), adjust the subject or message text (you may wish to remind them that this is simply an exercise!) and click **Send** to send the message.

3. To open the 6-2 Clubs reviewed.ppt presentation, which is in the MOUS PowerPoint 2002 folder, use the **File - Open** command, open the **MOUS PowerPoint 2002** folder then double-click the **6-2 Clubs reviewed.ppt** file to open it. If PowerPoint offers to merge this file, click **No**.

   To apply the changes made by Sandra Tyson to the subtitle of the first slide, use the tool button to go to the first comment. Click the check boxes for these changes **Inserted "Annual Report" (Sandra Tyson)**, **Deleted "Club activity" (Sandra Tyson)** and **Text format: style (Sandra Tyson)**.

   To save the presentation, click the tool button then use **File - Close** to close the presentation.

EXCHANGING DATA
Lesson 6.3: Working on the Web

EXCHANGING DATA
Lesson 6.3: Working on the Web

1 ▪ Previewing a presentation as a Web page

▪ Open the presentation that you would like to see as a Web page.

▪ **File - Web Page Preview**

The Web page opens in your default browser; you see it as it would appear if published on an intranet or the Internet. Two panes are created; an Outline pane in which you can select a slide and a Slide pane that displays the selected slide.

You can see neither the animations nor the slide transitions.

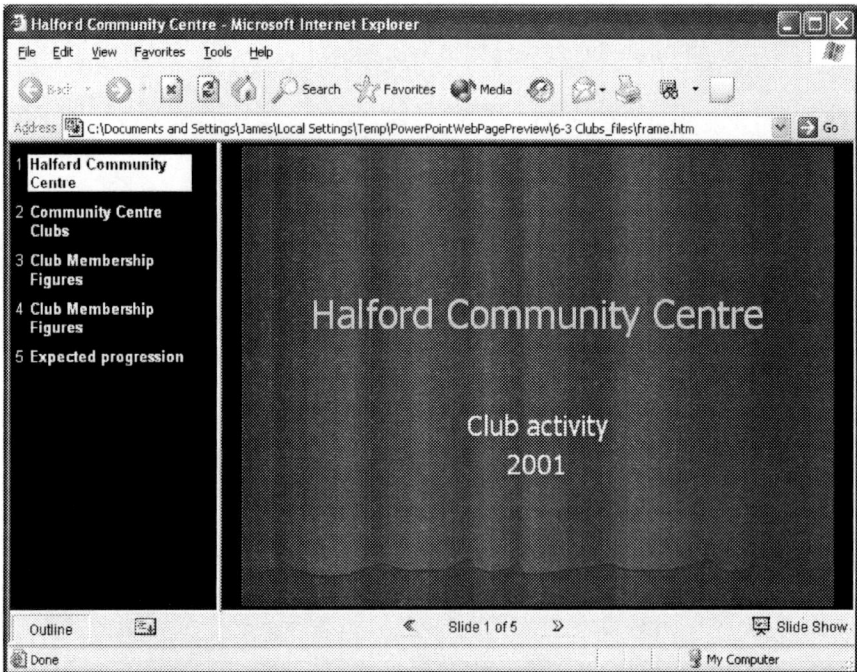

▪ To hide the Outline pane, click the **Outline** button at the bottom left of the window; to re-display this pane, click the same button again.

▪ To expand the outline, click the button; to collapse it, click the button.

*The **Notes** button can be used to hide or display the Notes pane. When a slide contains notes, the button is preceded by a white tick in a red check box.*

⁕ To go from one slide to another, click the slide name in the Outline pane or click the ⬚ and/or ⬚ button.

⁕ To return to PowerPoint, close the browser with the **File - Close** command.

📖2 ▪ Saving a presentation as a Web page

When you save a presentation as a Web page, you save it in HTML format so you can publish it on an intranet and/or the Internet. This type of presentation can be viewed in a Web browser, even if PowerPoint is not installed on the user's computer.

Saving a presentation as a Web page is not the same as publishing it on to a Web server. You may wish to save as a Web page even if you cannot publish from your computer.

⁕ Open or create the presentation that you wish to use for the Web page.

⁕ **File - Save as Web Page**

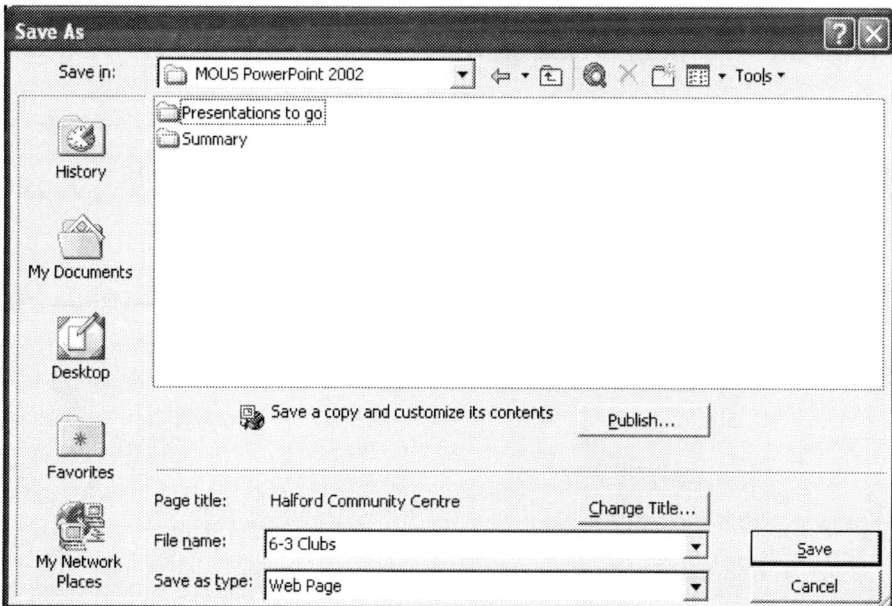

*The **Save As** dialog box opens on the screen. You can see that the **Save as type** list automatically displays the **Web Page** option.*

※ If necessary, enter a new name for the Web page in the **File name** box.

※ Click the **Change Title** button if you wish to change the page title then click **OK**.

The page title will appear on the browser's title bar.

※ Select the folder in which you want to save the Web page.

※ Click the **Save** button.

> *This creates a copy of the presentation.*
>
> *The presentation may contain components such as bullets, background textures, graphics; these are saved with the presentation, in a supporting files folder. This folder uses the same name as the Web page and is stored in the same folder. If you move or copy your Web page, remember to move this folder too, to preserve all its links with the Web page.*

3 ▪ Publishing a presentation on the Web

When you publish a presentation, you make it available to other users via an intranet or the Internet. If you want to publish your Web page onto an intranet, you need to save it into a Web folder, on a Web server. If you want to make the Web page available on the Internet, you should contact your Internet service provider to find out if and where space is available for publishing your presentation. If you do not have access to a Web server, you can always publish into any folder on a hard disk.

※ Open the presentation you wish to publish (or the Web page, if you have already saved it as one).

※ **File - Save as Web Page**

※ Enter a name for the Web page in the **File name** box.

※ Make sure that **Web Page** appears in the **Save as type** list box.

» If necessary, click the **Change Title** button to change the page title that will appear in the browser and click **OK** to confirm it.

» Click the **Publish** button.

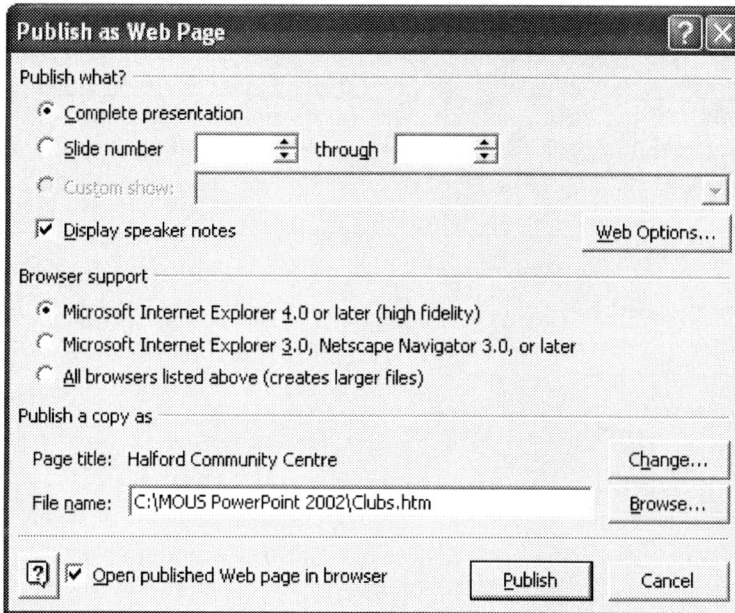

» Choose to publish the **Complete presentation** or choose the **Slide number** option and specify the range of slides you want to publish in the corresponding boxes.

» To display the speaker's notes for the presentation, activate the **Display speaker notes** check box.

» To enhance the look of the presentation in the browser, select the appropriate option in the **Browser support** frame.

» In the **File name** box, enter the location on a Web server or other computer in which you want to publish your Web page.

*You can use the **Browse** button to select this server location.*

» Activate the **Open published Web page in browser** option to preview your page as soon as you publish it.

▪ Click the **Publish** button.

A copy of your presentation is now available on the Web server you specified. All Internet and/or intranet users can view your presentation, regardless of whether or not they have PowerPoint installed.

📄 *PowerPoint publishes the Web page to the chosen server or folder and if necessary, saves the presentation as an .htm file and creates a supporting files folder. When this occurs, all the files relative to the Web page are stored on the chosen server; only the original presentation remains on your disk.*

To update a Web page once you have published it, go into PowerPoint and open the source file of the presentation you want to modify (not the copy that you published on the Web server). Make your changes and republish your presentation on the Web.

🔲4 ▪ Setting up an online broadcast

With PowerPoint 2002, you can broadcast a presentation on the Web. This is a way of showing the presentation to viewers in different locations. The presentation is saved in HTML format. The technique described here is designed for broadcasts to small groups (less than 10 people).
To broadcast a presentation with live video and sound, you must equip your computer with a video camera and microphone. You will have to specify your computer's audio and/or video settings and the location of the files you wish to broadcast.

▪ Slide Show - Online Broadcast - Settings

*You may see a message informing you that the required components are not installed. If this happens, insert your Office XP or PowerPoint 2002 CD-ROM in the drive and click **Yes** to install the feature.*

Broadcast Settings

Presenter | Advanced |

Audio/Video
- ○ None
- ● Audio only
- ○ Video and audio   Test...

Presentation display

Slide show mode: | Full Screen ▾ |

Presentation options
- ☐ Display speaker notes with the presentation

File location

Save broadcast files in:

| \\my_server\shared_folder | Browse...

Help   OK   Cancel

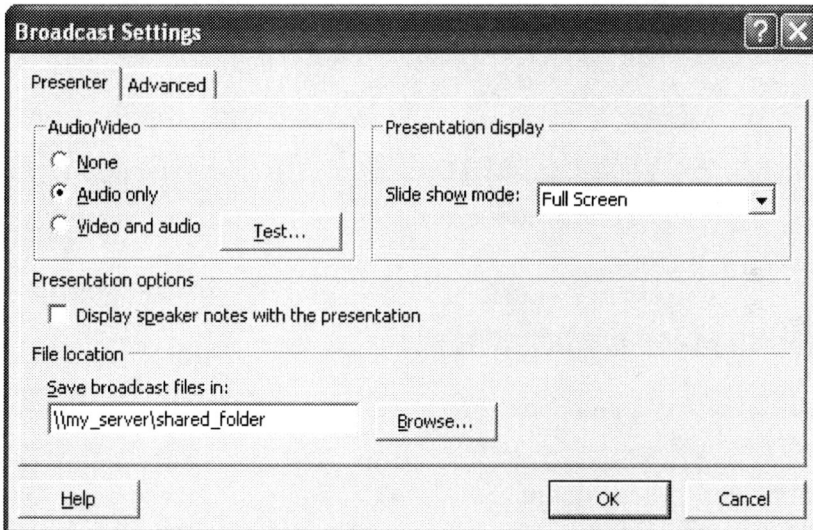

* Under the **Presenter** tab, choose the audio/video settings you want to use: **Video and audio** (if you have installed a camera and a microphone on your computer), **Audio only** (to use only the audio feature) or **None** (to use neither of these features).

The Audio only option ensures you use fewer of your computer's resources. The Test button runs a check on your installation.

* To display speaker notes to your viewers during the broadcast, activate the **Display speaker notes with the presentation** option.

* In the **Save broadcast files in** text box, specify the address of a shared folder on the server that will contain the broadcast files (use this type of format: \\server_name\share_name).

You have to use a shared folder so that your viewers can join the broadcast.

* Open the **Slide show mode** list and choose a display option for the slide show window during the broadcast: choose **Full Screen** to occupy the whole screen or **Resizable Screen** to allow easy access to other programs (such as Microsoft PowerPoint) during the broadcast.

* Click **OK**.

The **Advanced** tab can be used, among other things, to select a Microsoft Windows Media server (for broadcasts to more than 10 computers).

These settings will apply to all broadcasts from your computer. You should check these settings before each broadcast session to ensure that the appropriate options are active.

5 ▪ Making an online broadcast

You can record a broadcast (which users can then view at a later date), make a live broadcast or schedule one.

Recording a broadcast

When you record a broadcast, other users will be able to view at any other time in the future. The presenter should carry out this operation.

* Open the presentation you want to broadcast.

* Set up the broadcast, as required (cf. the previous section).

* **Slide Show - Online Broadcast - Record and Save a Broadcast**

You may see a message informing you that the required components are not installed. If this happens, insert your Office XP or PowerPoint 2002 CD-ROM in the drive and click **Yes** to install the feature.

* If necessary, modify the information shown in the **Record Presentation Broadcast** dialog box.

Record Presentation Broadcast

Please enter presentation information here. This information will appear on the lobby page.

Title:	Club report
Description:	A presentation of our club statistics
Speaker:	Adrienne Tommy
Copyright:	ENI
Keywords:	6-3 Club Report;Adrienne Tommy
Email:	Adrienne

Windows® Media Technologies

You can use PowerPoint to broadcast a live presentation to other users on your network. You can send slides, audio and video. A Web browser is used to view the broadcast.

Tips for Broadcast...

Settings...   Record   Cancel

*This information will appear in the lobby page of your broadcast. The **Title** box contains the name of the HTML file that will be created. The **Settings** button takes you to the **Broadcast Settings** dialog box.*

▪ Click the **Record** button.

If you are using a microphone or a video camera, your installation will be checked automatically.

▪ When any equipment testing is finished, click **OK** in the **Check** dialog box(es) that appear.

▪ In the **Broadcast Presentation** dialog box, click the **Start** button.

The slide show appears in the slide show window.

▪ At the end of the slide show, click anywhere to leave the presentation.

Microsoft PowerPoint

ⓘ Congratulations! You've completed the broadcast of your presentation. Your recorded broadcast is saved at the following location:

C:\MOUS PowerPoint 2002\6-3 Club Report.htm

Replay Broadcast   Continue

A message appears to confirm that you have recorded and saved your broadcast. It also indicates its location.

- Click the **Replay Broadcast** button, if you want to review your presentation in the browser window. Otherwise, click the **Continue** button.

📄 *If you want to see a recorded broadcast, open Internet Explorer and go to the shared folder that contains the broadcast files. Double-click the html page corresponding to the file created during the recording.*

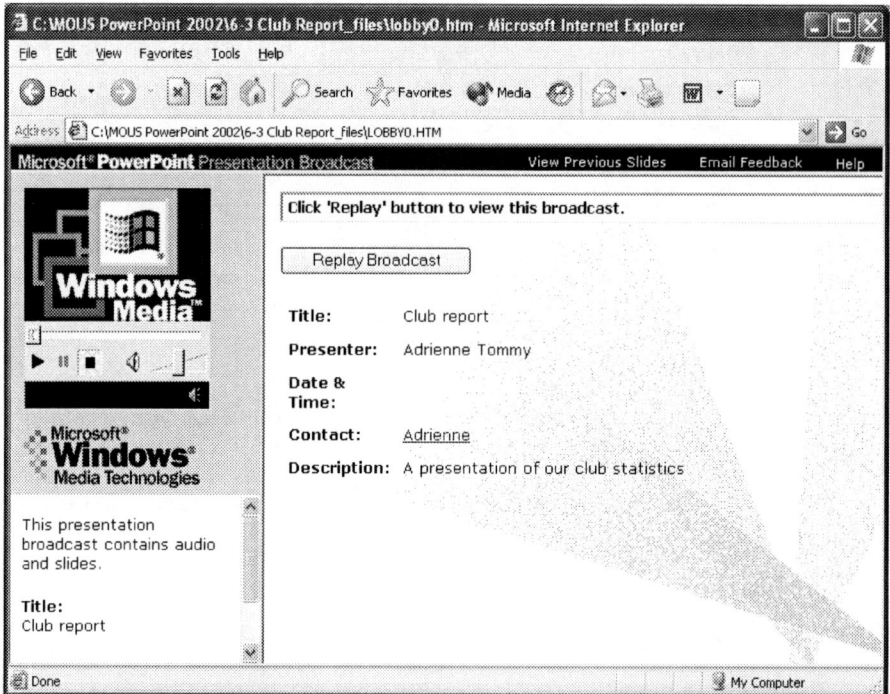

*An introductory page appears. A click on the **Replay Broadcast** button will start the presentation broadcast.*

Scheduling a live broadcast

Scheduling a live broadcast involves planning a broadcast for a specific time for a chosen group of viewers. To do this, you need to have access to e-mail.

- Open the presentation that you want to broadcast.
- **Slide Show - Online Broadcast - Schedule a Live Broadcast**

*You may see a message informing you that the required components are not installed. If this happens, insert your Office XP or PowerPoint 2002 CD-ROM in the drive and click **Yes** to install the feature.*

» In the **Schedule Presentation Broadcast** dialog box, enter the information you want to appear in the lobby page of your broadcast.

» If required, click the **Settings** button to change your broadcast settings.

» Click the **Schedule** button.

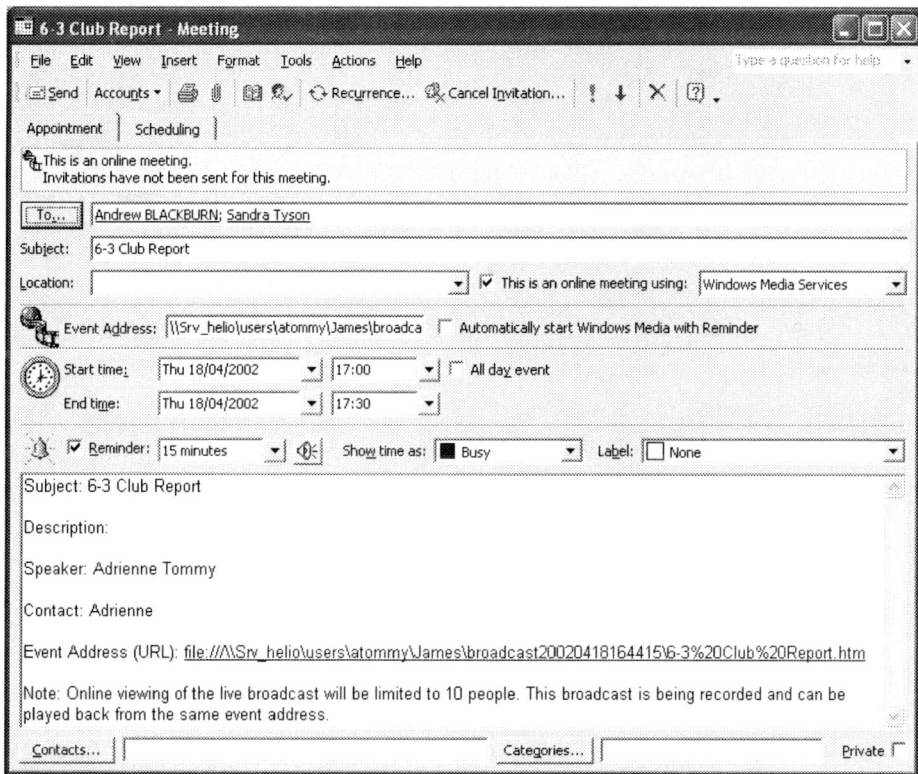

Your e-mail application starts.

» If you are using Microsoft Outlook, make a meeting request, as you would for any other meeting. If you are not using Outlook, enter the date and time of the broadcast in the message.

The URL of the broadcast site is automatically inserted in the body of the message.

» If necessary, click **OK** on the message informing you that your broadcast schedule was successful.

» Before the time at which you scheduled the broadcast to start, open the presentation with **Slide Show - Online Broadcast - Start Live Broadcast Now**.

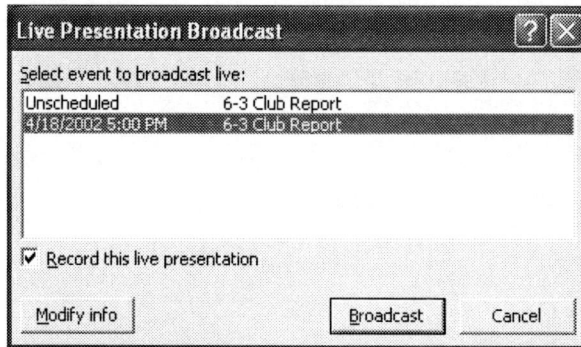

» When you are ready to start the broadcast, click the **Broadcast** button, click **OK** if any equipment check messages appear then click the **Start** button.

If you are using video and/or audio features, this equipment will be checked automatically before the broadcast is started.

» Click the **Start** button again to begin your live presentation broadcast, if you are starting it before its scheduled time.

If you are using video, remember that you will not be able to see yourself in the video display when you are making your presentation. Stay where you are during your presentation, to make sure you do not move out of the camera range.

*To reschedule your broadcast use the **Slide Show - Online Broadcast - Reschedule a Live Broadcast** command.*

Broadcast viewers will need Microsoft Internet Explorer 5.1 (or later version). It is advisable to join a live broadcast approximately 15 minutes before it is due to start. Open the e-mail application that contains the invitation to the broadcast and click the broadcast URL link.

Below you can see **Practice Exercise** 6.3. This exercise is made up of 5 steps. If you do not know how to do one of the steps, go back to the title that corresponds to that particular lesson. When you have finished, you can check your work by reading the **Solution** that follows.

Steps that are likely to be tested during the MOUS exam are marked with this symbol: ⊞. However, it is a good idea to complete the whole exercise to ensure you have understood everything covered in the lesson.

☞ Practice Exercise 6.3

*To work on exercise 6.3, you should open the **6-3 Clubs.ppt** presentation, which is in the **MOUS PowerPoint 2002** folder. The actions described in this exercise would normally be performed in a shared folder on a network, or directly on the Internet. However, many users may not have access to this type of resource. For this reason, you can carry out the actions below in the **MOUS PowerPoint 2002** folder.*

1. Preview the presentation as a Web page. Scroll through all the pages then close your Web browser.

⊞ 2. Save the presentation as a Web page in the **MOUS PowerPoint 2002** folder. Call the file **Clubs**. Change the page title into **Club report**. Close the Web page.

⊞ 3. Open the **6-3 Clubs.ppt** presentation again and publish the first three slides into the **MOUS PowerPoint 2002** folder; use the same file name proposed in step 2. Open your Web browser to view the published file. When you have seen it, close the browser and the presentation, without saving it.

⊞ 4. Open the **6-3 Club Report.ppt** presentation in the **MOUS Power-Point 2002** folder and set up an online broadcast (use only audio and display speaker notes). The broadcast files should be created in the **MOUS PowerPoint 2002** folder.

5. Record your broadcast. On the lobby page, the **Title** should read **Club report** and the **Description** should be **A presentation of our club statistics**.
Save and close the presentation.

If you want to put what you have learnt into practice on a real document, you can work on summary exercise 6 for the EXCHANGING DATA section, that you can find at the end of this book.

It is often possible to perform a task in several different ways, but here only the easiest solution is presented. You can go back to the corresponding lesson if you want to see other techniques you could use.

Solution to Exercise 6.3

1. To preview the presentation as a Web page, use the **File - Web Page Preview** command. To see each page, you can click the name of each slide.

   To close the Web browser, use the **File - Close** command.

2. To save the presentation as a Web page called "Clubs" in the MOUS PowerPoint 2002 folder, use the **File - Save as Web Page** command. Check that the **MOUS PowerPoint 2002** folder appears in the **Save in** box and that the **Save as type** option is **Web Page**. In the **File name** box, type **Clubs**.

   To change the page title, click the **Change Title** button and type **Club report**. Click **OK** then click the **Save** button.

   To close the Web page, click the ✕ button in the top right corner.

3. To open the 6-3 Clubs.ppt presentation, open the PowerPoint **File** menu and click the name of the presentation at the bottom of the menu. To publish the first three slides, using the same Web page file name as in step 2, use the **File - Save as Web Page** command again.
   Check that the **MOUS PowerPoint 2002** folder appears in the **Save in** box and that the **Save as type** option is **Web Page**.
   Type **Clubs** in the **File name** box.
   Click the **Publish** button. In the **Publish what?** frame, tick the **Slide number** option, click the first text box and type **1** then click the second text box and type **3**. Make sure the **Open published Web page in browser** option is active and click the **Publish** button.
   Click **Yes** to replace the existing **Clubs.htm** file.

If you wish, look at each page then close the browser by clicking the ☒ button in its top right corner.

Close the presentation by clicking its ☒ button and click **No** on the message that prompts you to save the presentation.

4. To open the 6-3 Club Report.ppt presentation in the MOUS PowerPoint 2002 folder, use **File - Open**, browse to open the **MOUS PowerPoint 2002** folder, if necessary, and double-click the **6-3 Club Report.ppt** file to open it.

To set up the presentation for an online broadcast, use **Slide Show - Online Broadcast - Settings**.
If PowerPoint needs to install a component, click **Yes** on the message and follow the instructions.
Make sure the **Audio only** and **Display speaker notes with the presentation** options are active. In the **Save broadcast files in** box, give the file path for the **MOUS PowerPoint 2002** folder, if necessary. Click **OK**. If a message appears to tell you that this folder is not shared, click the **Continue** button.

5. To record an online broadcast, use **Slide Show - Online Broadcast - Record and Save a Broadcast**.
In the dialog box that opens, click the **Title** box and type **Club report**. Next, click the **Description** box and type **A presentation of our club statistics**.
Click the **Record** button.

When all the tests are carried out, click **OK** as many times as necessary to close the **Check** dialog boxes.

Click the **Start** button on the **Broadcast Presentation** dialog box.
Let the presentation run then click at the end to exit it.
On the last dialog box, click the **Continue** button.

To save and close the presentation, click the 🖫 tool button and use **File - Close**.

SUMMARY EXERCISES

SUMMARY EXERCISES

Open the **Summary 1A.ppt** presentation, which is in the **Summary** folder within the **MOUS PowerPoint 2002** folder.

Go to Slide Sorter view.

Apply a **Title Slide** layout to the first slide in the presentation.

Save the changes made to this presentation.

Leave this presentation open and create a new presentation based on the **Profile.pot** design template.

Save this new presentation as **Summary 1B.ppt** in the **Summary** folder within the **MOUS PowerPoint 2002** folder.

Copy slides 2, 3 and 4 from the **Summary 1A.ppt** presentation and paste them after the first slide in the new presentation you have just created (**Summary 1B**).

Delete the first slide in **Summary 1B**, which is a blank slide.

On all the slides in the presentation, display the text **Rich Chocolate Cake** in the footer.

Print the presentation, ensuring that the three pages print on the same page.

Save the changes you made to this presentation.

Solutions to both presentations are saved as **Solution 1A.ppt** and **Solution 1B.ppt**, in the **Summary** folder.

Open the **Summary 2.ppt** presentation, which is in the **Summary** folder within the **MOUS PowerPoint 2002** folder.

Enter text into the second slide, according to the illustration below:

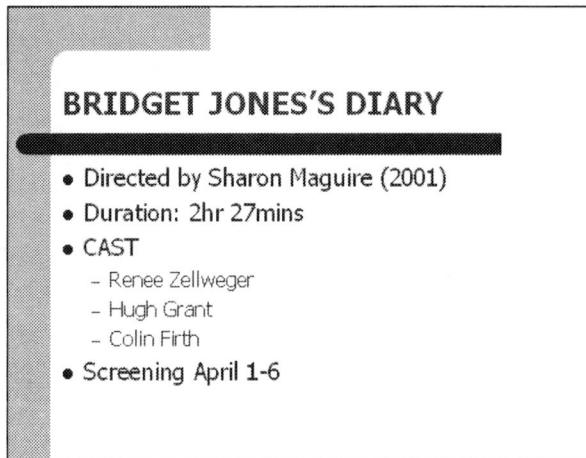

BRIDGET JONES'S DIARY

- Directed by Sharon Maguire (2001)
- Duration: 2hr 27mins
- CAST
  - Renee Zellweger
  - Hugh Grant
  - Colin Firth
- Screening April 1-6

On the first slide, change the text "SHELDON CINEMA" to **SHELDON CINEMA CLUB**.

Check the spelling of the entire presentation.

Find the word "Length" and replace it with **Duration**.

On the first slide, apply the **Tahoma** font to the text **THIS MONTH'S FILMS** and increase the font size to **28**.

Replace the **Arial** font by the **Tahoma** font on all the slides.

On the fifth slide, apply bold type and a purple font colour to the text **SCREENING TIMES**.

On the fifth slide again, change the colour of the bullets on the existing paragraphs; apply the aquamarine colour, instead of black. The paragraphs are currently centred; align them on the left.

SUMMARY EXERCISES

On the fifth slide again, apply a **1 line** spacing before the body text paragraphs. The solution to this exercise is saved as **Solution 2.ppt** in the **Summary** folder.

Summary Exercise 3   USING TEMPLATES

Open the **Summary 3.ppt** presentation, which is in the **Summary** folder within the **MOUS PowerPoint 2002** folder.

Apply the **Profile.pot** design template to all the slides.

Using the slide master, apply the **Lucida Handwriting** font to all the slide titles (if you do not have this font, apply another of your choice).

Apply the first colour scheme offered in the **Apply a color scheme** list; apply this to all the slides in the presentation.

Edit the chosen colour scheme and change the **Accent** colour to yellow (instead of scarlet).

Apply the pattern called **Plaid** to the background of all the slides.

The solution to this exercise is saved as **Solution 3.ppt** in the **Summary** folder.

Open the **Summary 4.ppt** presentation, which is in the **Summary** folder within the **MOUS PowerPoint 2002** folder.

On the first slide in the presentation, draw a rectangle and enter this text in it: **Water Sports in Trinidad**.

Using the available AutoShapes, draw the boat shown on the picture below:

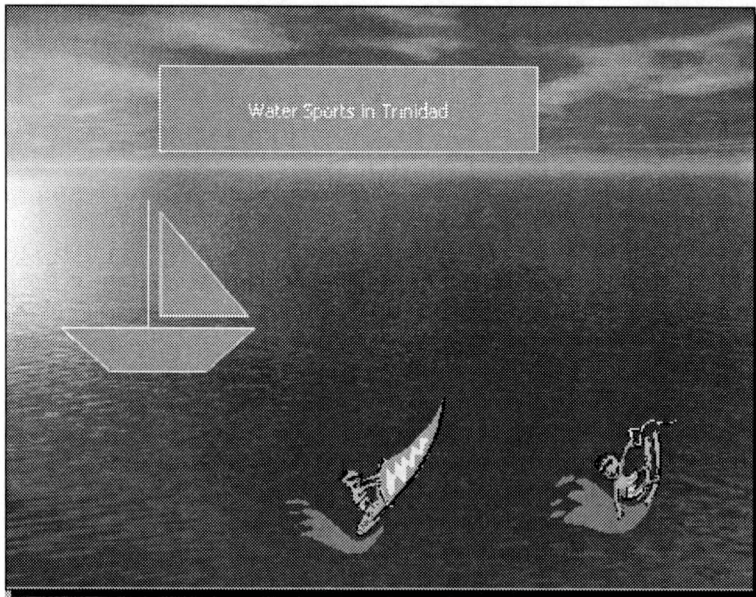

Group the shapes that make up the boat.

Apply the preset gradient called **Daybreak** as a fill to the rectangle containing text and to the boat shapes.

Delete the rectangle containing text that you created at the start of the exercise.

In its place, insert the following WordArt object (do not hesitate to move or resize this Word Art):

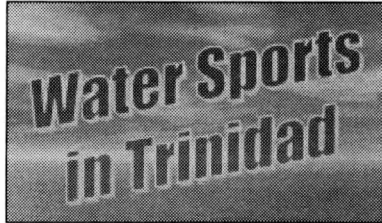

Stay in the first slide and insert the picture called **Diver.wmf**, which is in the **Summary** folder within the **MOUS PowerPoint 2002** folder. Move it to the bottom left corner, next to the windsurfer.

Rotate the picture of the waterskier slightly, in a clockwise direction.

On the last slide, insert the following table and apply the required formatting:

The solution to this exercise is saved as **Solution 4.ppt** in the **Summary** folder.

Open the **Summary 5.ppt** presentation, which is in the **Summary** folder within the **MOUS PowerPoint 2002** folder.

Apply the animation scheme called **Dissolve in** to all the slides in the presentation.

On the picture of the diver on the first slide, apply a **Spin** emphasis effect that will occur after the previous effect.

Change the order of the animation effects so the two effects applied to the diver occur first.

Preview the animations on the first slide.

On the picture of the windsurfer, insert a hyperlink that takes you to slide 4 (add a ScreenTip if you wish).

Run the slide show and let it continue until the end.

Set timings on all the slides so each slide stays on screen for 10 seconds.

Apply a **Blinds Vertical** transition effect, accompanied by a **Breeze** sound, to all the slides.

The solution to this exercise is saved as **Solution 5.ppt** in the **Summary** folder.

Open the **Summary 6.ppt** presentation, which is in the **Summary** folder within the **MOUS PowerPoint 2002** folder.

Insert the following data from the **Summary 6.xls** Excel workbook, without creating any links:

- insert the table into the fourth slide in the presentation,

- insert the chart into the fifth slide.

You can resize or move these objects, if necessary.

Change the first comment on the presentation, replacing **Add some waffle to this slide** with **Add more text to this slide** then delete the second comment.

If you wish, send this presentation by e-mail for review by a friend or colleague of your choice.

Preview this presentation as a Web page.

Save it as a Web page, using any file name you like and publish it into a folder or Web server, if you have access to one.

The solution to this exercise is saved as **Solution 6.ppt** in the **Summary** folder (there is no solution for the Web page).

<table>
<thead>
<tr><th colspan="5">MICROSOFT POWERPOINT 2002
Table of objectives</th></tr>
<tr><th>Tasks</th><th>Lessons</th><th>Pages</th><th>Exercises</th><th>Pages</th></tr>
</thead>
<tbody>
<tr><td colspan="5">Creating presentations</td></tr>
<tr><td>Create presentations (manually and using automated tools)</td><td>Lesson 1.1 Titles 6, 7,9</td><td>26 and 29</td><td>Exercise 1.1 Points 6, 7, 9</td><td>35</td></tr>
<tr><td>Add slides to and delete slides from presentations</td><td>Lesson 1.2 Titles 4, 6 and 7</td><td>46, 49 to 51</td><td>Exercise 1.2 Points 4, 6 and 7</td><td>53</td></tr>
<tr><td>Modify headers and footers in the Slide Master</td><td>Lesson 1.2 Title 8</td><td>51</td><td>Exercise 1.2 Point 8</td><td>54</td></tr>
<tr><td></td><td>Lesson 1.3 Title 3</td><td>60</td><td>Exercise 1.3 Point 3</td><td>66</td></tr>
<tr><td colspan="5">Inserting and modifying text</td></tr>
<tr><td>Import text from Word</td><td>Lesson 2.1 Title 6</td><td>77</td><td>Exercise 2.1 Point 6</td><td>85</td></tr>
<tr><td>Insert, format, and modify text</td><td>Lesson 2.1 Titles 1, 2, 4</td><td>70, 74, 76</td><td>Exercise 2.1 Points 1, 2, 4</td><td>84 and 85</td></tr>
<tr><td></td><td>Lesson 2.2 Titles 1 to 9</td><td>92 to 102</td><td>Exercise 2.2 Points 1 to 9</td><td>103 to 104</td></tr>
<tr><td colspan="5">Inserting and modifying visual elements</td></tr>
<tr><td>Add tables, charts, clip art, and bitmap images to slides</td><td>Lesson 4.2 Title 1</td><td>164</td><td>Exercise 4.2 Point 1</td><td>172</td></tr>
<tr><td></td><td>Lesson 4.3 Titles 1, 2, 6 and 7</td><td>178, 182, 189 to 191</td><td>Exercise 4.3 Points 1, 2, 6 and 7</td><td>199 and 200</td></tr>
<tr><td>Customize slide backgrounds</td><td>Lesson 3.2 Title 7</td><td>132</td><td>Exercise 3.2 Point 7</td><td>137</td></tr>
<tr><td>Add OfficeArt elements to slides</td><td>Lesson 4.1 Titles 1, 2, 8, 9 and 11</td><td>144, 145, 150, 151 and 155</td><td>Exercise 4.1 Points 1, 2, 8, 9 and 11</td><td>158 and 159</td></tr>
</tbody>
</table>

Tasks	Lessons	Pages	Exercises	Pages
Apply custom formats to tables	Lesson 4.2 Titles 3 to 10	166 to 170	Exercise 4.2 Points 3 to 10	173
Modifying presentation formats				
Apply formats to presentations	Lesson 1.2 Title 3	44	Exercise 1.2 Point 3	53
	Lesson 3.1 Title 1	108	Exercise 3.1 Point 1	111
	Lesson 3.2 Titles 1, 2, 3, 5 and 6	116 to 121, 126 to 128	Exercise 3.2 Points 1, 2, 3, 5 and 6	137
Apply animation schemes	Lesson 5.2 Title 2	223	Exercise 5.2 Point 2	233
Apply slide transitions	Lesson 5.1 Titles 7 and 8	213 to 215	Exercise 5.1 Points 7 and 8	216 and 217
Customize slide formats	Lesson 3.2 Titles 1, 3, 5 and 6	116, 121, 126 and 128	Exercise 3.2 Point 1, 3, 5 and 6	137
Customize slide templates	Lesson 3.1 Title 2	109	Exercise 3.1 Point 2	111
	Lesson 3.2 Titles 1, 2, 3, 5 and 6	116 to 121, 126 to 128	Exercise 3.2 Points 1, 2, 3, 5 and 6	137
Manage a Slide Master	Lesson 3.2 Title 8	133	Exercise 3.2 Point 8	138
Rehearse timing	Lesson 5.1 Title 6	210	Exercise 5.1 Point 6	216
Rearrange slides	Lesson 1.2 Title 5	47	Exercise 1.2 Point 5	53
Modify slide layout	Lesson 1.2 Title 3	44	Exercise 1.2 Point 3	53

TABLE OF OBJECTIVES

Tasks	Lessons	Pages	Exercises	Pages
Add links to a presentation	Lesson 5.2 Title 5	230	Exercise 5.2 Point 5	233
Printing presentations				
Preview and print slides, outlines, handouts, and speaker notes	Lesson 1.3 Titles 2 and 4	58 and 63	Exercise 1.3 Points 2 and 4	66
Working with data from other sources				
Import Excel charts to slides	Lesson 6.1 Titles 1 to 4	238 to 244	Exercise 6.1 Points 1 to 4	246 and 247
Add sound and video to slides	Lesson 4.3 Titles 4 and 5	184 and 188	Exercise 4.3 Points 4 and 5	199
Insert Word tables on slides	Lesson 6.1 Titles 1 to 4	238 to 244	Exercise 6.1 Points 1 to 4	246 and 247
Export a presentation as an outline	Lesson 2.1 Title 9	82	Exercise 2.1 Point 9	86
Managing and delivering presentations				
Set up slide shows	Lesson 5.1 Title 1	204	Exercise 5.1 Point 1	216
Deliver presentations	Lesson 5.1 Titles 2 and 3	206 and 207	Exercise 5.1 Points 2 and 3	216
Manage files and folders for presentations	Lesson 1.1 Titles 3, 5 and 8	19, 26 and 27	Exercise 1.1 Points 3, 5 and 8	35
Work with embedded fonts	Lesson 1.1 Title 10	31	Exercise 1.1 Point 10	36
Publish presentations to the Web	Lesson 6.3 Title 2	263	Exercise 6.3 Point 2	273
Use Pack and Go	Lesson 1.1 Title 11	32	Exercise 1.1 Point 11	36

Tasks	Lessons	Pages	Exercises	Pages
Workgroup collaboration				
Set up a review cycle	Lesson 6.2 Title 2	253	Exercise 6.2 Point 2	259
Review presentation comments	Lesson 6.2 Titles 1 and 3	252 and 255	Exercise 6.2 Points 1 and 3	259
Schedule and deliver presentation broadcasts	Lesson 6.3 Titles 4 and 5	266 and 268	Exercise 6.3 Points 4 and 5	273 and 274
Publish presentations to the Web	Lesson 6.3 Title 3	264	Exercise 6.3 Point 3	273

INDEX

A

ALIGNMENT

ANIMATION

ANIMATION SCHEME

APPLICATION

ARROW

AUTOSHAPE

B

BACKGROUND

BORDER

BROADCAST

BULLET

C

INDEX

D

E

L

LAYOUT

LINE

LINK

M

MASTER

MERGING

MICROSOFT POWERPOINT

MOVIE

MOVING

MULTIMEDIA

N

NORMAL VIEW

T

List of available titles in
the Microsoft Office User Specialist collection

Visit our Internet site for the list of the latest titles published.
http://www.eni-publishing.com

ACCESS 2002
ACCESS 2000
EXCEL 2000 CORE
EXCEL 2000 EXPERT
EXCEL 2002 CORE
EXCEL 2002 EXPERT
EXCEL 2003 CORE
EXCEL 2003 EXPERT
OUTLOOK 2000
OUTLOOK 2002
POWERPOINT 2000
POWERPOINT 2002
WORD 2000 CORE
WORD 2000 EXPERT
WORD 2002 CORE
WORD 2002 EXPERT
WORD 2003 CORE
WORD 2003 EXPERT